re.CL....ng
A Handbook for Developing a Restorative Culture in Your Church

RENOVATE
Publishing Group

J. Pete Tackett

&

Michael D. Stover

Endorsements

While reading this book, I kept thinking to myself, "I wish I had had a team around me to help me recover when I fell." There have been a couple of times in my life when life as I knew it came to a screeching halt. One instance was out of my control, the other was because of me "running red lights," as Pete talks about in this book.

While I had the prayer support of my loving wife and a few brothers in Christ to help me recover, I believe I would have benefited greatly from the approach Pete lays out in this book. As a teenage boy who went through a church split over the actions of the pastor, I felt then that he was being treated poorly, but there was no team to support or encourage him back to spiritual health. Since then, I've had a heart for those who have fallen and I feel the importance of Biblically restoring fallen brothers and sisters.

Too often, we Christians are quick to reject the wounded rather than loving them back into spiritual health. Please pray about whether or not you will allow God to use you to be a welcoming, safe place for fallen brothers and sisters, and to be part of a team to restore them to spiritual health.
Thanks again for sharing!!

Bob Hickling
Celebration Director
Tiftarea Celebration with Will Graham
Billy Graham Evangelistic Association

re.CLAIM.ing - A Handbook for Developing a Restorative Culture in Your Church deals with the very real problem of spiritual and moral failure among Christian leaders and laity. No believer is exempt from the temptation to become selfish, self-centered, and self-reliant while ignoring the pleading of God's Spirit and the caring people that God has placed around them. The book offers its readers an honest portrait of how even the most dedicated Christian can fall into a destructive pattern of behavior and experience a public "failure." Thankfully, it also offers the hope of renewal and a process for restoration for those willing to commit to a season of dedicated introspection and growth.

The greatest value of the book is found in giving a healthy church that is committed to being a house of restoration a process it can follow to help struggling people find their way to wholeness, as well as fruitfulness in ministry. The author's story is living proof that it can happen!

Steve Holt
Church Services Director, Tennessee Baptist Mission Board
www.tnbaptist.org

I've been in ministry for over 60 years, and I just wish I'd had Pastor Pete Tackett's book MANY YEARS EARLIER! I've always had a heart for restoring the fallen, but did not have a tool like this to help me do restoration work, and to lead the churches I pastored to have a culture of restoration.

In fact, I served on Pastor Pete's Restoration Team—and I praise God for the happy outcome of his story—but I (and each of us on his team) felt so unprepared to do restoration work; IF ONLY back then there had been a tool like his book! This is a pastoral epistle: it comes from the heart of a pastor and clearly guides pastors in how to lead the church into a restoration ministry.

It's a personal story; Pastor Pete tells his flame-out (and come-back) experience honestly, transparently, and does not sugar-coat it. (I was there, and he tells it exactly as it happened.) This book is powerful; it shows the transforming power of a church willing to do the 'messy' work of restoration and willing to adopt a restorative culture!

And re.CLAIM.ing is also a very practical book. It doesn't only inspire the reader to help churches LAUNCH a ministry to fallen servants of the Lord, it shows step-by-step how to IMPLEMENT it. I recommend this book to any pastor or layperson wanting to help their church become a safe haven for the broken minister or church leader.

Mike Dawson, CoachingServants.com

Seasoned church revitalization veteran Pete Tackett handles the difficult task in Church Revitalization and Renewal that few if any want to tackle.

In Pete's latest book, *re.CLAIM.ing - A Handbook for Developing a Restorative Culture in Your Church*, the author deals with the issue of restoration. Specifically, he deals with restoring the broken in a broken world. Some ministers break themselves while others are broken by the churches they lead.

Buy this book and read it first quickly. Then, after a few days of reflection, reread this book with a pen and pad in hand. You will find incredible insight and unmatched passion in the heart and words of the author.

Restoration of the minister regardless of the reason is a difficult task. Tackett has been given the strength and fortitude to walk along side of fallen ministers through the task of reclaiming and restoring the minister of the gospel. Some pastors in revitalization find themselves in the midst of despair due to the incredible challenges they face in seeking restoration for the local church.

Pete Tackett develops and champions a restoration culture designed to help ministers get healthy again and stay healthy. Sometimes the church is the one wounded and the authors confront their challenges head on with a spirit of expectancy that the Lord can bring renewal to the local house of God.

Tackett declares, "A major reason pastors and churches have not embraced the idea of restorative ministry is that we get fixated on those pastors who have made big mistakes and committed big sins, and we think restoration is about giving them a pass. We do not recognize the variety of needs among pastors and see the incredible opportunity God has given us to rescue His wounded soldiers."

I have had the privilege of seeing the author at work in his field of restoration and am so thankful that there is one who will do the hard stuff. Pete leads out in this endeavor and there is none better.

Tom Cheyney, Founder & Directional Leader
Renovate National Church Revitalization Conferences
The Renovate Group

It is my joy to enthusiastically and wholeheartedly commend *re.CLAIM.ing - A Handbook for Developing a Restorative Culture in Your Church* by Pete Tackett and Michael Stover. It is a practical handbook helping churches and ministry leaders build a culture of safety, compassion, and mending for those that find themselves at a place of brokenness.

But the most captivating aspect of *re.CLAIM.ing* is the personal stories of these dear friends. They have "been there, done that, and gotten the t-shirt." Their compelling personal stories add solid credibility to the thesis of the book.

The story has blessed and inspired me. It has affirmed the direction of the ministry I lead to focus on and invest in the total health of our network of pastors and ministry leaders.

Randy C. Davis
President & Executive Director
Tennessee Baptist Mission Board

Published by The Renovate Publishing Group
ISBN-13: 978-1951340032

Acknowledgements – J. Pete Tackett

No one gets to the finish line writing a book about any subject without the help and encouragement of lots of people and I am no different. I have many to thank and even in doing so, will doubtless leave off some that should be included, but I am going to try.

First, I must thank God for not only salvation and a lifetime of blessings but also for not giving up on me when many others did.

I am beyond blessed to have a beautiful and godly wife, Lori, who walked in the valley of pain and through the season of restoration with me. She and my daughter, Sarah, and son, Jonathan, along with his wife, Kelly, are like bedrock to me and I would never have even attempted this book without their affirmation and affection.

I am grateful for a church like Antioch Baptist Church in Johnson City, Tennessee, that not only is willing for me to lead a restorative ministry but actively walks in the journey of restoration with me. They willingly let me be gone several weeks to get the writing done and prayed me through to completion. I am grateful for our deacons and leadership team for their enabling and encouraging of this project as well.

I am thankful for our staff, Aaron Cox, Lewy Cornett, Elizabeth Bowles, Richard Long, and Mike Cohran, plus others that have come and gone on that team who helped shape the ministry of restoration and healing at Antioch and for the willingness of the team to do my job many times so I could go away and write.

I will be forever grateful for men who led my own journey of restoration and from whom I learned much of this: Dale Ledbetter, Stan Breeden, David Forrester, and Mike Dawson, along with all my friends at First Baptist Church of Columbia, Tennessee.

Finally, my life has been immeasurably enriched spiritually and professionally by the Pastors who have shaped me: Robert Foster, P. J. Scott, Don Strother, Kenneth Kyker, and Mike Dawson. If you listen carefully, you will hear their voices in the pages of this book. Thank you men, and may your tribe increase!

Acknowledgements – Michael D. Stover

When Pastor Pete approached me about co-authoring a book with him on this topic, I was both excited and hesitant. Excited because, intellectually and spiritually, I know firsthand that God can use even our tragedies and failures to create beautiful masterpieces. But hesitant because the personal pain and consequences of our upheaval in ministry were still very fresh and evident. They still are at this moment.

Therefore, I must acknowledge my gratitude to Pastor Pete for including me in this project. He sought to leverage my professional writing skills; but I also firmly believe that he sought to engage me in the process of personal restoration. And although I have not been through the formal process laid out in this book, the writing and wrestling it entailed have truly been transformative for me, and for my wife. Thank you, Pete, for your compassion and wisdom.

I must also thank my wife for reliving those painful experiences with me again and again as we wrote, prayed, commiserated, and let go of those people and events. We are not completely whole; we may never reach that blessed state. But we are closer to wholeness than we have ever been.

Others believed in me even when I did not, even in the cruel aftermath of our implosion, and let their support be known. A close circle of friends loved me and prayed over me continually, and for them, I will always be grateful. I am here today because of them. Larry Murphy and Joe McIntyre remain powerful friends and influences in my life. Pete Tackett joined their ranks when we moved to Northeast TN, as did Pastor Chris Miller and many of the church family at Northridge Community Church, West Market Street Campus.

All five of my children have never ceased to believe in me, even when they did not understand what has happening, or when times were rough. Each of them were forced to sacrifice much in their own way due to my ministry crisis, and each rose to the occasion. Pray with me that healing will restore their broken hearts and draw them back to close fellowship with God and His church.

My extended family has never wavered in their support, providing a safe haven in which to live and begin picking up the pieces. They are as thrilled as I am to see this book come to fruition, as a sign that God is still at work in and through me. Thanks to my parents, David and Lynn Stover, my sister Angie May and husband Wayne, and Haley and Jake. My father-in-law, who only recently passed away, never wavered in his encouragement or support. Thank you Walter Pickering, and Carolyn, for your unconditional love that is so like that of our heavenly Father.

Several mentors from past years also deserve mention. Their words from the past, and their stellar examples, kept me from turning completely away from the faith in my darkest moments. Pastor Roy Yelton, Pastor Roger Stockton, Dr. B. Gray Allison, Dr. Michael Spradlin, Dr. Dale Ellenburg, Dr. Ronnie Mayes, and Dr. Robert J. Pittman; God used your words and influence to steer me through dark days. Thank you.

CONTENTS

FOREWORD

So, you've turned to the foreword. In my observation, "foreword people" fall into one of two categories. First, they either want a synopsis of the content and a benefit analysis of the book in order to decide if it merits their time to read it; or second, they find themselves already persuaded and wish to gain context for the maximum effect as they peruse the pages. Whichever category you fall into, I seek to answer both of these motives.

In order to do so, let me tell you my story with Pete. Three years ago he was unknown to me personally, but had invited me to lead conferencing on prayer in his church. At some point during my time there, he began to tell me of his journey and the restoration ministry the Lord had given him. As I listened with rapt attention, something began stirring in my heart. The more he shared, the more I began to see that what God had given him was far more than any personal benefit he had received or for those whom he had taken through the process. Instead, at some point, I cried out something to the effect, "Pete, you have to write this down in a book! Do you know how many churches could benefit from the practical handles God has given you on how to restore people who've fallen in sin?! Do you realize that there is no process out there that helps churches do this? Instead, our church fields are strewn with the carnage of brothers and sisters in Christ shipwrecked by moral failures, and with whom we have no idea what to do. We have no clue how to practically obey Galatians 6:1."

Later Pete would confess to me that he rather ignored our conversation for a year or so, but others began to echo the same sentiments when they witnessed the work of God through him. Eventually, he began to understand God was giving him an expanded assignment. When God paired him up with Michael, the pieces fell into place that have resulted in the book you now hold in your hands. I am so excited because I anticipate the great benefit that will result for so many pastors to help restore their members overtaken in a trespass. I can only imagine the church cultures that will result, in which the grace of God deals with sin in such a way that people are neither left unaccountable nor cast away.

So, having said these things, please allow me to highlight the four benefits that most stood out to me as I perused this manuscript; four benefits that I trust you will also find equally beneficial.

MY FAVORITE FOUR BENEFITS OF THE BOOK

1. It addresses an unaddressed need.

I already referred to this earlier, but it bears repeating again. Galatians 6:1 (NIV) commands us, "Brothers, if someone is caught in a sin, you who are spiritual should restore him gently. But watch yourself, or you also may be tempted." The Bible clearly instructs us that we are to restore a fallen brother or sister ensnared in sin, yet thousands of our churches have no practical idea how to do this. A gaping hole exists between God's command and our obedience; this book addresses that. For this first reason alone, you will benefit from it.

2. Its practical-ness gives you concrete handles you can use.

Pete and Michael do not write out of theory. Rather, the forges of real-life experience have smelted and hammered out practical tools that you can implement in your own church. They have developed principles, a plan, and clear action steps for people wishing to shepherd a brother or sister overtaken in a trespass. They do not merely state that restoration should take place, but equip you how to do it practically where the rubber hits the road – personally my favorite part of the book. For this second reason alone, but especially coupled with the first, you will benefit.

3. Its balance gives you a well-rounded understanding of restoration.

In writing about theological foundations related to restoring a fallen brother or sister, they respectfully acknowledge that varying opinions exist on the subject. The effect of evenhandedly recognizing the views of other Christians in a spirit of humility as they advocate for their own position gives a richer and fuller understanding of what the Scripture teaches on the subject. For this third reason, you will benefit.

4. Its authenticity helps you have proper expectations. Pete and Michael's authenticity runs in two directions. First, they are transparent about their own personal journeys and how God worked through those to shape the book. As you come to know them through their stories, you gain a fuller sense of what they are advocating and why.

Second, they not only tell the success stories of those for whom the restoration process worked out gloriously, but also the stories of people who did not continue in the restoration process and fell away. By presenting both sides, they give a holistic picture of the good and the bad, the successes and failures, the way people responded or didn't, which proves of great value in setting realistic expectations for the kinds of things that will happen in your own setting. For this fourth reason, you will benefit.

A FINAL WORD

As you can readily see, I'm excited about their work. Yet in addition to their book, there remains one more reason for which I'm equally excited. Realizing that many people reading this book will desire further help, they have set up a website with additional practical aids. Even now as of the writing of this foreword, they are developing material, video clips, blogs, and other tools to be of benefit to you. No doubt as this ministry progresses, the Lord will grant additional resources not thought of yet. If you are interested in exploring their website, go to www.reclaimingbook.com.

In Christ,

John Franklin
Founder and President
John Franklin Ministries - A Ministry to the Local
Church for Revival and Spiritual Awakening
Clarksville, Tennessee
www.johnfranklinministries.org

Introduction

If you are a pastor at heart and love words like most of us do, there are phrases that grab your attention, worm their way into your soul, and become what one author calls an axiom. Axioms are those sayings that become filters and decision-making tools. Once that thought or phrase works its way into your soul, it makes some decisions much easier. One such axiom in my life started out as a casual note while listening to a sermon in 1986.

Dr. Jess Moody, then pastor of First Baptist Church in Van Nuys, California, was speaking to the State Evangelism Conference in Nashville, Tennessee (Do you even remember when that was a thing?). He was under fire for his unorthodox, and at that time, controversial way of reaching out to the community around him. In particular, he had been attacked in the press and especially in denominational publications for allowing the "ungodly" actors and actresses from Hollywood to participate and lead in his church.

As he told the story, he uttered a phrase in passing that went largely unnoticed, but I wrote it down. I don't recall consciously meditating on it or thinking about it. Truthfully, in my early days of ministry, thinking and meditating was not something I did much at all. Yet, in the coming years, this little phrase began to shape my ministry and my heart for broken and hurting people, especially broken and hurting ministers and lay leaders.

That phrase was simple. He said, "Some churches are pitchers and some are catchers. I want the church I serve to be a catcher!" As best I can remember, that is a direct quote. This was long before you could go back and watch or read every word someone said on the Internet.

In the years since, when given a chance to extend mercy or rain judgment, my default position has shifted toward mercy. I say shifted because none of us are perfect at this, and the closer we are to the person who is broken, the more likely we are to choose judgment. Yet with each passing year, hearing those words ringing in my ears and in my soul, I have tried to err on the side of helping those who are messed up and those who have messed up.

Little did I know that 20 years later, I would find myself among the broken and needing a pastor or a church to be a catcher in my life. In chapter one, you will be invited into that story, plus the story of my friend and co-author, Michael Stover, who found himself broken by some of the very people he served. He, too, needed a church that would choose to be a catcher rather than a pitcher.

Unfortunately, we both discovered during those difficult days in each of our lives that there are lots of loving pastors and lay people in churches across all denominations, many of whom want to help the broken, but have no idea how. Other churches and pastors are afraid to get involved because of traditions and power structures within their churches and denominations, and judgment from those outside. We also discovered that there were almost no local churches that had an established plan to restore the broken and the fallen. The ones who do are overwhelmed by the need, and the waiting list is often too long for the person who is hurting now.

After years of casually reaching out to hurting, fallen, and broken leaders, I was astounded at the lack of resources and help when I needed it. The further I got into this process, the more I realized that while I had cared about the broken and fallen, I had never really developed a system for caring for them. I had been a friend, a shoulder to cry on, a safe place to vent, but there was no process for helping them get back on their feet emotionally and spiritually. I am deeply indebted to my pastor and friend Mike Dawson, and a group of good friends (Stan, David, and Dale), who were willing to get in the mess of my life and develop a process on the fly to help me get back on my feet.

As a result, I entered a painful year of oversight and accountability through which I learned for the first time of sins that I did not recognize in myself; how my performance-based ministry had cheapened the grace of God and shortchanged my family; and how to recognize red lights that God was putting in front of me. While in the process, I did not enjoy it. Yet, even though it was not a perfect process and was incredibly painful at times, it gave me a track to run on and people to coach me. It would not have been enough for them to let me cry on their shoulders or vent my pain. There had to be a process that caused me to evaluate and change, forgive and seek forgiveness, and rest and recover.

When I left the church where I served as pastor, I had no intention of ever returning to vocational ministry. In fact, I told everyone who would listen that I "would never again be out on the point of the spear, where I could be so easily attacked." To be sure, I did not quit God or the church. In fact, my wife and I attended church the week after my resignation and every week thereafter. I did not, however, intend to ever again be a pastor.

Months into that process, God showed up on my patio one morning as I was reading and praying and said, "It is time for you to get back to work." Like Abraham and Sarah, I laughed, questioning who would have me and if I even was willing, how would I go about getting back to work in the church. After a fairly combative time of prayer and thought, I began to seriously understand that there would be a second wave of calling and ministry in my life. At that time, I did not understand that it would be housed in a local church where I would once again be "on the point of the spear;" but I knew it would be a more focused effort on being a "catcher" rather than a "pitcher."

A little over two years later, I accepted the permanent call to lead a small, broken church that I had been leading through a transitional phase. During that season, God reminded me that He was looking for a church that would be a safe haven and that would be actively pursuing restorative ministry. There was never a vote or even much conversation - we just began to love people that had been broken by our church and other churches, and we tried to help them in practical ways. Over the next three years, we fumbled and stumbled our way into developing a church culture in which restoration is routine and there is a process in place to make that happen.

By telling my story via the Internet and through Men's Conferences, we began to attract broken people in increasing numbers. Some were former lay leaders in their churches who got run over by a power structure; some were the power structure. Others were pastors and ministers who had failed at marriage or management or people skills, while some were pastors and ministers who were railroaded by a shadow government in a church they served. What they all had in common was deep pain and a common idea that God may not be through with them, but they were through with his church. In the coming chapters, with their permission, we will tell you some of their stories. Some of the stories have happy endings and some do not. Some will be the real names and some will be disguised.

Beginning about three years ago, some people I look up to, like John Franklin, Tom Cheyney, and others, began to tell me I needed to put this in writing. I do not live to publish as some do, but I do live to see the broken and fallen restored; therefore, I have finally decided to do so. The purpose is not to tell my story or Michael's story, or even Antioch's story, but to help that pastor or church leader who wants to be a "catcher" to create a culture and develop a process in their own church, so when the time comes, they can be not only a friend, but a real source of restoration.

To that end, the book is in three sections. The first will address the need and theological foundation of restorative church ministry. The second will share ideas and resources for helping your church create a culture where restoration is the default position for those who are hurting. Finally, we will deal with a core process that can be adapted to specific needs as they arise. Thanks for reading!

res·to·ra·tion

/ˌrestə'rāSH(ə)n/ *noun* 1. the action of returning something to a former owner, place, or condition.

"Brothers, if anyone is caught in any transgression, you who are spiritual should restore him in a spirit of gentleness. Keep watch on yourself, lest you too be tempted." Galatians 6:1

Chapter 1

A Necessary, but Thankless Ministry

We are broken people, and we live in a broken world. Any book about restoring the broken has to start there. It is not only the fallen pastors who make headlines that are broken. All of us are broken to some extent. For some, the brokenness looks worse than it does in others. For a few, it remains a secret brokenness that never bursts its way into the public arena, or that public brokenness is still a way down the road. That brokenness can be caused by our sin, pride, and our own spiritual stagnation. For others, their brokenness is caused by the very people they felt called to serve - they were blindsided not by sin, but by people, circumstances, and personal attacks in the church.

Whatever the reason, there are thousands of pastors, staff members, and former lay leaders in our churches who are, in the words of the Apostle Paul, "shipwrecked."

While much of this book will be for and about vocational ministers, that brokenness does not stop at the stage or in the church office. The people in the pews are also broken and living life in a broken world. Laity, or whatever word you use to describe the non-clergy, are as messed up as broken pastors and ministers. Eerily similar to the situations when pastors find themselves broken, when a deacon, choir member, trustee, or small group leader find themselves publicly humiliated by the results of poor decisions, sinful habits, or just being in the wrong place at the right time, the church typically has no idea what to do with them.

Let me say it again. We are broken people living in a broken world, and the church by and large has no idea what to do with broken people. I found that out the hard way. We are about to introduce you to the authors and tell our stories.

1

For me (Pete), I failed. As I weave my story through this book, I want nothing to be construed as an excuse for sin, a justification for acting out, nor a reason for my flameout. For Michael, he was broken by the church he served. Our stories are different, but we both wound up at the same place — needing a hand up and finding resources for healing sorely lacking in the local church, especially the ones accessible to us.

Pete's Story

In the fall of 2007, I (Pete) had the world by the tail. I had "outkicked my coverage" in the football vernacular and was pastoring a church that had grown from about 600 when I joined their staff to a weekly average of around 1,100-1,200, with occasional gusts up to 1,400. The first few years I had served as a staff pastor and part of the leadership team, and for the last four years as lead pastor. We had a great staff of people who loved God, loved each other, and loved the lost. It was like any other small town First Church, a mixture of people and attitudes, but was by and large a very grace-filled and graceful church. They loved me and my family and treated us well. As in any church, there were those that did not like my style, but even most of them were gracious about it. There is nothing I am going to say in this book that should in any way be construed as critical of that church. Not only did they love me before I crashed, but when I fell, they still loved me; and even though they had no idea how to do it, they helped restore me. A year after I left the church, as I prepared to go teach in Africa for a season, that same church held a going away reception for me. As I said, life was good.

As long as I can remember, I have suffered from what doctors refer to as SAD, Seasonal Affective Disorder.[1] It is a

---

[1] National Institutes of Health Website.
https://www.nimh.nih.gov/health/topics/seasonal-affective-disorder/index.shtml. Accessed June 17, 2020.

mild form of depression that typically is driven by the shorter days, grayer weather, and general dreariness of the winter months. I am not a medical professional, so if you want more details, you will have to find them elsewhere. By 2007, I had grown accustomed to it and knew what to expect, and even had some tools in my box to use to overcome it and stay functional. I had taken antidepressants on one occasion in the 1990s to try to avert it on the advice of my doctor. It did not help much and caused a lot of other problems, so I just learned to deal with it.

In the late summer of 2008, it hit especially hard and especially early. I did not recognize right away that it was happening, although my wife did. She was and is very protective, so almost from the beginning, she was encouraging me to go to a doctor. Because of some family history and my own (unknown to me at the time) prejudices about mental illness, I rebelled against that idea, thinking to myself, "Who is going to follow a pastor who is not spiritually strong enough to overcome depression?"

I did not know until I finally blew up and melted down, embarrassing myself, my family, and my church, that she was not necessarily talking about a psychiatrist, but just wanted me to go to my primary care doctor to make sure something physical was not happening. The realization of this misunderstanding many months later caused me to understand how far gone I was, even in the early stages of this battle. It was not just the depression, but I had allowed myself to get so busy and so self-reliant spiritually that I was exhausted all the time, not taking care of myself physically, spiritually, or emotionally. At this point in the journey, I was not even listening to my wife, my soul-mate, and the one person on earth who loved me unconditionally and always saw the best in me. It would prove to be a disastrous decision. I was like a weak animal, cut off from the herd, isolated, and at the mercy of the predator.

It came to an end with one horrific week and one particularly awful night as I considered suicide, alcohol, and running away. God gave me several opportunities that night to turn to him, but I did not. I have no excuse for that. He finally intervened when a police officer pulled me over and I had a misdemeanor charge of patronizing a known area of prostitution and drugs. This is not a book about me, so I won't spend pages telling the story; but if you want to know more than I cover here, my life is an open book and you can go to www.petetackett.com and watch a video of me telling that story. Even though that was many years ago, I leave the story up online because almost every month, someone stumbles across it and reaches out to me for help. It is still painful to tell, but it is part of my story and all things do work together for good to those who love God and are called by Him.

I will tell you more of that story as we progress further through the book together; but for now, let me introduce you to my friend and co-author, Michael Stover. Mike's story is vastly different from mine. While no one is perfect and all of us make mistakes, Mike's story is not one of needing restoration because of an act of sin or failure in his own life. His story is all too familiar, especially in my denomination. It is a story of what happens when someone is broken not by their own decisions, but by the decisions of a church they serve.

Michael's Story

I (Michael) was well into my second year after winning a serious battle with cancer, and in my eighth year of a growing pastorate, when a larger and more influential church in my local association came calling. They were in a period of transition, with a trained transitional pastor, after their former pastor of over twenty years retired. As the search team shared with me, things had stagnated over the last several years. After a process of prayer and investigation involving the congregation, they sought a younger pastor (I was then 38) who would be willing to do things differently. I distinctly remember being excited about the phrase "outside the box" being used frequently in our meetings. They desired a pastor who could lead them to do whatever it took to reach the surrounding communities. At the time, the church already had two innovative community outreach initiatives in operation, so I felt confident they were open to new avenues of ministry.

After prayer and consideration with my wife, we moved to that church and I became their senior pastor in February 2009. Things did not, however, go as we had hoped. As we sought to lead and grow the church, and enjoyed some success, it slowly became like swimming against a hidden rip current. After only four years, while my family and I were on vacation (the first vacation we could afford in well over a decade), church leaders met to discuss how to get rid of us. After we returned, I was confronted in a meeting with the two senior deacons and not only asked to resign, but was specifically told to lie about being asked to resign.

I readily admit to making mistakes as a pastor, at times allowing zeal to surpass good sense. I did not do everything right. I offended some people and made apologies. As much as I tried, some families simply did not care for me. I believe part of the problem was the large dichotomy between myself and the former pastor. We were in no way alike, although we were at the time long-time friends, and I still hold a great deal of respect for him. In spite of this, there were victories, measurable progress, new believers baptized, and many being discipled and engaged in ministry. The week before our family vacation, I met with a representative of the local Baptist university to discuss how their ministry students could be used in our branch campuses. They actually wanted their students to learn from us how to innovate and take church to local communities to reach them for Christ.

At no time did the deacons or any church member raise a single allegation of misconduct against me. During my meeting with the deacon leadership, I repeatedly asked why they felt I should resign. They only repeated that they felt a change was needed. Since that time, certain stories have been circulated to explain my departure. I believe they were an effort to cover up the truth of what really happened. Some people I knew in ministry believed the stories. Many more did not and told me so, anguished over what happened to us.

I was effectively blackmailed into lying about the reason for my resignation. Knowing that we had just returned from vacation and our family funds were low, I was threatened with being dismissed with no severance pay whatsoever unless I lied. I was instructed to tell the congregation that my resignation was my own choice and I simply felt it was time to move on. I was not to whisper the truth to anyone.

We lived in the church's house and were 400 miles from the rest of our relatives. We literally had no place to go. For my family's sake, I felt I had no choice but to comply. To force the issue publicly would split the church and leave us homeless and penniless. I resigned, gave the required 30-day notice, and preached on Sundays for a month while we packed our belongings. Many in the church came privately for an explanation, but I could not share the truth. I had to get my family back home. A few who knew what happened behind the scenes expressed private support, even gave us money to help with the move; but no one was willing to stand publicly and decry what had happened.

In July 2013, at age 43, we (myself, my wife, and four children, aged 19, 17, 10, and 8) moved across the state and into a three-bedroom, one-and-a-half bath home that we shared with my parents. Our oldest child, a daughter, was left behind working a new job that she could not leave. My wife knew the truth, but our kids only knew we had worked hard, only to be kicked out into the street. They privately asked their mother what I had done. Raised in the church, they couldn't believe a church would kick us out without a good reason. Over half of my severance pay was used in moving back to familiar surroundings, where we at least had a place to live. I had no job, no home, no prospects, and absolutely no desire to ever set foot in a church again.

Where Do You Find Help?

When I (Pete) began to unravel in the fall of 2008 and especially into the early months of 2009, I began to reach out to various people and organizations for help. To be sure, I let my pride keep me from talking to most of the people I was closest to, but I did seek help. At one point, I confided in a co-worker how hard it was getting to face life each day. He was sympathetic and concerned, but said he had no idea how to get help for me.

The night I finally had my public meltdown I had gathered my staff that afternoon and told them I needed a break, and for very good reasons, none of them could cover for me when an emergency came up that night. I spoke with some pastor colleagues and each was sympathetic, but had no concrete process to help. I contacted my denomination and found out their pastoral care department had been downsized out of existence at that point, although they have since seen the need to restart it.

A national ministry often advertised on the radio about their extensive counseling ministry for hurting and broken ministers so I reached out to them, only to find out that they had a great two-week program that would only cost me $10,000 — money I did not have. One of our denomination's greatest leaders has a ministry that takes in broken preachers, but when I called, there was a 13-month waiting list. In my pride and fear of becoming known by those closest to me, I overlooked some resources that were available, but everywhere I did look, there was a dead end.

Anecdotally, since we began to aggressively pursue restorative ministry, I have asked hundreds of small church pastors, of which I am one, if they have a specific process in place to help the broken and fallen. While all of them have in one way or another said they hoped they would be able to help and they were very open to helping, so far, not one has been able to produce a written and adopted and field-tested process of restoration. In speaking with one national leader who has 60,000 churches connected to his network or database, I asked how many he knew of that had a core plan in place. He looked at me and said, "One!" and pointed to me! I don't necessarily believe there is only one in his network, but it does illustrate the rarity of this concept.

It took me a year or two for the fog to clear, but when it did, I realized what I should have known and been implementing all along in my own ministry. That is, the most fertile ground for meaningful restoration is the local church. Paul, in his writing to the church at Galatia, said, "*Brothers, if anyone is caught in any transgression, you who are spiritual should restore him in a spirit of gentleness. Keep watch on yourself, lest you too be tempted.*" (Galatians 6:1)

Thus, 16 months after I left the ministry, much to my surprise, I found myself contemplating taking on the pastor role at a hurting church. I decided if this was indeed God's will, it would have to be a church that was proactive in seeking out the broken and creating an atmosphere that loved and deliberately attempted to restore the fallen. I knew it would require specific processes and that we would need to learn how to do this well. It has been a work in progress, but we have learned some things that work and some things that do not. Hopefully, what we have learned will give you a head start that was not available when our journey began.

The Importance of a Restoration Culture

I have no idea why you are reading this book. It may be because you already have a friend or parishioner who is in need of restoration, and you have no idea where to start. It might be because you have seen the effects of an unforgiving church on a friend or family member. It might be because you are overwhelmed with the number of hurting people you meet who have been used up and tossed aside by the church, a place that should be the safest place on earth for a believer. I doubt seriously, though, if you are thinking it might soon be you in need of a helping hand. I hope you are right and that you can remain a practitioner of restorative ministry without ever having to experience it firsthand yourself.

If you do, however, it behooves you to build into your church a culture of safety, healing, and restoration. The time to develop a culture and install a process of restoration is not when you or someone in your church family needs it. It is hard to build an ark while the storm is raging. Our Florida friends say, when you are up to your waist in alligators is not the time to discuss draining the swamp.

At the church I served, we tried under both the former pastor and myself to develop a balance of grace and truth. We worked hard to make it a place where hurting people could come without judgment, taste the grace of God, and hear the teaching of God's Word without fearing rejection or condemnation. No church is perfect, but by the time I needed it, there was a healthy atmosphere of love and forgiveness. What we did not have, though, was a process of restoration.

In retrospect, what I have come to call a culture of restoration is really most important. If a church is healthy and understands that Jesus came preaching both grace and truth (John 1:17), and is trying to be a place where both are displayed and cultivated, you can develop and implement a process. If you have a process but the culture is unforgiving, or has been developed by a tradition that believes once someone fails, God is through with them, it will be much harder. It is not impossible, but it is difficult. That is why one entire section of this book is devoted to the issue of culture.

The great irony of restorative ministry is that almost all churches will tell you when asked, that they are a "loving and welcoming" church. When specifically asked, most church members would say the atmosphere of their church is one of forgiveness. Yet, when a lay leader who has been respected by the church and has provided invaluable service and leadership to the church for many years fails at his marriage, finds himself in the news for a white collar crime, or just lets his reputation be tarnished by a moment of public disgrace, they almost always wind up leaving the church. Too often, they leave saying that grace was not available to them after all they had done for the church. When a long-tenured pastor has an affair, or his wife leaves him unexpectedly, or when his son does something to traumatize the church, they don't feel that love, welcoming spirit, and forgiveness; and more often than not, they leave not only that church, but church in general.

These are not numbers borne out by a large, scientific study, but from our limited experience over the past nine years. We found only half of those who suffer failure and are rejected by their church meaningfully re-engage with a local church in the five years following that event. Additionally, only about one in three will walk through a restoration process and then re-emerge in the next five years on a church staff or pastoring a church. Too often, these broken servants of God just become part of a recently defined church demographic called "the chronically de-churched." Even when they attend church, they are often on the fringe, just showing up and attending large gatherings, but rarely using the gifts God placed in them at their new birth and that they have spent a lifetime honing to serve the body of Christ, the local church. Think of that! Among both the broken and discarded laity and clergy living in our neighborhoods and walking around among us there are incredible gifts, talents, and abilities the church needs to grow and advance the Kingdom. But we either knowingly or in ignorance have discarded them, and we often do it in the name of the Savior who said, "a bruised reed, I will not break" (Matthew 12:20). These men and women are children of God, in need of redemption and the need to feel useful and wanted again. The church is lacking in servants to carry out the ministries God has assigned it. If the church could mine this rich vein of resources and restore the fallen, everyone wins.

Now, for the graceful among us, this is a place where things could really get out of hand fast. After all, you already have a heart to see people healed and you see the needs in your church, and so you just pick those folks up off the side of the spiritual highway and immediately put them back to work. You really do more damage than good when that happens, because without a specific process of restoration that addresses sinful patterns, bad habits, blind spots, and broken relationships, you are setting that person up to fail again. There is a reason the Bible cautions us against quickly laying hands on someone (I Timothy 5:22).

When the Church is Wounded

One of the trickiest parts of restorative ministry is how to help when the church has been wounded. What if the offender was a deacon, elder, pastor, or small group leader at the church where you are trying to implement restorative ministry. Churches in general have a heart to restore the

11

broken in theory. We spend thousands of dollars each year in ministry projects to reach those "out there" who are broken, addicted, or overtaken in a fault. We have no qualms about welcoming with open arms a prodigal son who has been away from the church for years or who flamed out in another church, offering hope, counseling, accountability, and resources. What about the leader, though, who has hurt THIS church? It is so much harder when you have been doing life with that leader and now they have failed. For whatever reason, it is easier to restore those we don't know than to stand with those we do know.

What do you do when he or she stands before the church and repents, says "I am sorry," and asks for forgiveness? Too often, the church leadership is not equipped for that moment. Leaders need to be prepared to direct the church to offer forgiveness while at the same time offering accountability. Leadership needs to know the balance of providing a restorative process to the offender and protecting the sheep.

Normal reactions to that moment are extreme. On one hand, we accept the apology and pretend nothing ever happened. In that case, the offender is on his own to figure out what went wrong and how to fix it. At the same time, the church, many of them wounded to different degrees, don't feel safe addressing their pain. The other extreme is saying to the offender, "We don't ever want to see you or think about you again!" As an aside, that is usually the response of a toxic church even when the leader did nothing wrong and the church has wounded or offended them. They don't want him or her around reminding them of their sinful actions.

We will address this more fully in the process phase, but this is the place for mature, spiritual discernment. There are times when it is acceptable for former leaders to remain in the church while going through the process; but in most cases, they need to seek out another fellowship while they work their way back to wholeness. For now, let me say that the wider the influence of the broken or offending party, the less likely it is they can stay around initially. However, don't misunderstand me. I believe the most effective church to offer restoration is the one where the person has been serving.

In my case, I did not understand it at the time because my entire life was tied up in the church I had just left. I wanted to just go to my community group and attend worship, but my Restoration Team said no. In retrospect, at that moment, I did not know what I did not know. I thought I could be there and be objective and not cause any tension. In hindsight, I know they made the right decision. If I had stayed there, I would have surrounded myself with my supporters and might never have completed the process. There were things I learned deep into that journey that would never have been revealed to me if I was in the midst of what I considered to be my people.

More importantly, at that point, I did not realize the spiritual impact my sin and brokenness had wrought on hundreds of people who loved me and would have followed me anywhere. They needed time apart to deal with their grief and learn to love the pastor God brought to them. Having me in the room could have slowed or damaged that process. Ten years later, I am in touch with many of those close friends. But at the time, it was wise for them to have me go to another church, even though the offended church had ownership of my restorative process.

Do People Even Want Help?

Unfortunately, many of the broken are afraid or unwilling to engage in that kind of process, so they just stay on the side of the road unless a broken church or organization offers them a return to their previous roles without any work on their part. Many of us broken have our self-worth and identity tied up in our ministry roles, so we are desperate to get back on stage or back to work so we can feel better about ourselves.

Before my crash, I often said there is little difference between who I am and what I do. While that sounds noble, it is unhealthy for the pastor to not have some separation between what they do for God and who they are in Christ. In the years since then, I have tried to slow down enough to keep some separation between those two things, although even now, I have days when I think I have let Pete become completely absorbed in the role of Pastor Pete. Because that is true of many of us, especially those who have become unhealthy and out of balance, we want to shortcut the process. Hear this —there are no shortcuts in restoration ministry!

For others, ministry is not only a calling, it's their livelihood; so they can't afford to sit out a year for restoration and spiritual rehabilitation, or at least they think they cannot. Many of us have done nothing in our lives but work for the church in vocational ministry, and we think we have no marketable skills for the secular world. Therefore, we cover up our sin, ignore the core issues that led to the failure, and take the first ministry job that opens up. We do so at the cost of living a life of fear of people finding out about our past, or harboring our own faults in hopes we can control them and not let them overtake us again.

This is one of the places longtime vocational ministers struggle in their faith. It is hard for them to believe God can provide their needs, whether it is a marketplace job, a more affordable lifestyle, or the ability to do a variety of things to provide for their family. During the 16 months I was away from vocational ministry, I worked as a courier, wrote for some websites, and did whatever job I could to make ends meet. Even in my darkest hour, I never saw the "righteous forsaken nor His seed begging for bread" (Psalm 37:25).

I tell you this because if you are contemplating doing the hard work of developing a culture and process of restoration in your church, you need to know it is never fun and people are not lining up to do it.

When I (Pete) was going through my process, one of the requirements established by my team was that I would not speak publicly, take on any ministry role, or offer any pastoral counseling during the process without the permission of the restoration team. I chafed under that, especially when a friend called me about three months into the process and asked me to preach the funeral of his mother. I wanted to do it, but the team said no. It was difficult for me and for that family, but being willing to put yourself under the authority of a restoration team is a valuable exercise for ministers who may often have had some soft accountability in theory, but in practice, have almost none. Whether a person returns to vocational ministry or not, learning to sit under authority is worthwhile for ministers, especially those of us who are broken.

Before You Move On

Now that you have read a little of our stories, and seen an overview of the often missing ministry of restoration in the local church, you have a decision to make. It is hard work. It is not always successful. In fact, it is unsuccessful more often that it is successful. People in your church won't always like it. People that need restoration will struggle to understand why they have to go through the process. Yet the Scripture says if your brother is overtaken in a fault, the spiritual ones among you should gently restore him. Are you ready?

For Further Thought:

1. Can you identify one or more seasons in your own life when you would have benefitted from a process of restoration, even if your brokenness was not public?

2. Who have you seen leave leadership in the church that would have benefitted from a more proactive ministry of restoration?

3. List some pastors and churches you know of that are doing restoration well and note the unique approaches and processes they use to fulfill Galatians 6:1.

Chapter 2

More Than You Think

Restoration is a word that is fraught with baggage. It means something different to each of us. For some, it sounds like a "get out of jail free" card for someone who hurt us badly and does not deserve it. For others, it is a theological concept that has no practical application in today's church. For some, it conjures up bad memories of people who wounded them and then apparently got off scot free and moved on to another position of power, where we secretly wonder if they are doing it again, whatever *it* is or was.

Those in need of restoration harbor desires that it might somehow make them feel useful again. For almost all those in ministry, the word restoration is tied to the failures of those in vocational ministry and thus, does not seem to be that much of an issue, especially if there is no one in your orbit right now who has failed and needs restoration. Our collective experience over the past ten years underlines that it is more than you think, and that right now, in almost every church, someone is sitting in need of a positive and proactive ministry of restoration.

I think this collective misunderstanding of both the scope and need of restoration is rooted in what I call the "ick" factor. We rebel against helping people through these ugly episodes and seasons in their lives because in the back of our minds, we think that they did this to themselves and it is a mess we don't want to get into. Quite honestly, some of the sins that mar people's lives these days are just distasteful, and to get into the mire and muck with them makes us feel a little dirty, almost like we are condoning their actions or giving them a pass. Nothing could be further from the truth.

We will talk in some other places about the specifics of that, but restoration is not about giving anyone a pass or validating sinful thinking. It is about rescuing broken people and reclaiming some of the gifts that God has given to the church and that Satan has tried to steal. Furthermore, much of the restoration that is needed in the local church has nothing to do with huge public sin.

Consider if you would some of the following case studies of real people who have crossed our paths in the past ten years. I tell you their stories with their permission and in most cases, the names are real. Don't get fixated on who they are, but recognize that these same people, with different names and circumstances but the same issues, are sitting in your church and living in your neighborhood.

The Spiritually Depleted

John is what most of us would call a traveling evangelist. That is not really what he does because he focuses more on spiritual renewal than outreach, which makes his need both ironic and frightening. If a man with this much passion for prayer and renewal could find himself feeling dry and empty, what hope is there for me?

He had committed no sin; there was no coming earthquake of revelation that he had had an affair, embezzled money, or harbored any kind of secret life. When he came to speak to my church, he immediately responded to an offhand remark I made about needing to meet with someone who was currently going through the process of restoration in our church. He was so interested, in fact, that he asked to meet with me the next day to discuss it.

He spoke quietly and humbly of years spent on the road speaking to churches and conferences out of the overflow of his own prayer life and how God had used his story to encourage pastors and churches to seek God. It was clear to me and anyone who listened to him that these were not theories to him, but a ministry born of love for the Lord and His church. Yet, he said he was just "dry." Many years ago, another pastor friend said to me about his prayers that it seemed as if "the heavens are brass and my prayers are bouncing back to me." What both of them were saying is that they were out of gas, depleted of spiritual energy, and struggling to feel the connection to God that had been their lifeline for so many years.

These men did not need the same kind of restoration that one who has fallen into public sin needs, but John helped crystalize a thought in me that had been rolling around in the back of my mind for a long time. That is, there is a need for the local church to develop a culture of restoration that will recognize leaders, both laity and clergy, that are burning out, and have a plan and process to take them out of service for a brief time to renew their energy and recharge them, and then put them back into service. To use a sports analogy, there is a reason professional ball players come out of the game for a while. Coaches and GMs know there is no way a player can perform at their best if they play every single play.

While John was not a member of my church or yours, if you think about it a minute, you will recognize the depleted servants in your church. They are the once vibrant, fulfilled, and smiling servants who loved to rock babies so their parents could be taught the word of God. They are the spiritually gifted teachers who lived to open the Word of God to people so they could grow into fully devoted followers of Christ. They are the servants who were first in line when a need was announced so that the work of the church could move forward. And they are staff members who were once fully engaged, on the edge of their chairs, and leaning into the next ministry opportunity, who now have hollow eyes and seem to be asking the question, "Do I have to be there?" instead of "Do I get to be part of this?"

We use the word "burnout" too freely these days, but that is the best way to describe these precious servants. The way you restore them is more about atmosphere, appreciation, and culture than process, but the first step is recognizing the need for a break. If the church does not have a plan and an atmosphere that allows for recharging their batteries, you will look around one day and they will be gone, again robbing the church of valuable resources.

The Spiritually Defeated

Closely akin to the spiritually depleted are the spiritually defeated. Bill was an old friend who I had not seen since I left the area 17 years earlier. It was Christmas Eve and I had dropped by our local mental hospital to visit a lady in the midst of early onset dementia to let her know we still loved and cared for her. As I walked down the hallway, a voice called out to me, "Pastor Pete?" I turned and looked at an old man who obviously knew me, but I did not know him. As I walked toward him, he reminded me who he was. I was shocked. Bill was a shell of the man I had known when I was the youth pastor to his children. I could not have picked him out of a lineup had my life depended on it, and I had once been very close to his family.

With tears, Bill said he was in trouble at the very core of his existence and that he needed help. I tried to be compassionate but firm, knowing from his children some of the mistakes he had made. I told him that I had never met a man in prison or in a psychiatric hospital that didn't say they wanted to change, but few of them actually do when they get out and have a little freedom. I told him to call me when he got out and if he still wanted help, I would do everything I could for him.

Bill had once been a vibrant, effective lay leader in the church I was now pastoring. He was the kind of guy you tapped to lead a fundraising campaign — driven, aggressive, effective, and effusive. If he told you he would make it happen, it happened. He was national sales director of a bedding company and on the boards of various local ministries and non-profits. He got connected to a mission project in Romania and made many trips there, and raised thousands of dollars to build small chapels in rural villages after the fall of communism.

Not much shocks me anymore, but seeing Bill in that place and in that condition rocked me to my core. If Bill was susceptible to this kind of failure, it could happen to anyone. Bill did call me when he got out and we met. He told me a story of a life filled with doing big things for God for so long, that he let the busyness for God become his god. Coupled with what seems like a direct spiritual attack because of his effectiveness for the Kingdom, this busyness became his undoing. He contracted an illness, got hooked on prescription painkillers, sunk into a life of immorality, was divorced by his wife, and estranged from his children. By the time we met at the hospital, he had added alcohol to his painkillers and it nearly killed him physically. When I think of Bill's story, I think of the first half of John 10:10, "The thief comes only to steal and kill and destroy...."

Bill's story does not end well. In the ensuing months, Bill was under the watchcare and supervision of a Restoration Team made up of old friends from the church and a close Christian friend from another church. He worked his way slowly, sometimes reluctantly, but always meticulously through a process we laid out for him. He was making progress, beginning to sense the presence of God again, sober, making amends to his adult children, and sharing dinners and conversation with his ex-wife when he died unexpectedly, eight months into that process.

Yet, this untimely death is, in my opinion, not the tragedy of this story. As we walked with him during those months, old friends and former pastors as well as people he taught in Sunday School and those who went on mission with him told me repeatedly that they saw Bill falling and had no idea how to help him. They said things like "Bill was not himself," and "I was so worried about him but did not know how to talk to him." Because Bill ran with lots of spiritual leaders, each assumed someone else was investing in him and could talk to him. The result is that a man who had given his life and much of his money to the Kingdom had little or no support, and certainly had no one courageous enough to confront him and offer him a lifeline. I know that Bill, like all of us, is ultimately responsible for his own decisions, but the church and the parachurch ministries he was aligned with did not have a plan in place to rescue the lost sheep. The real tragedy of Bill's story is that he dried up spiritually while surrounded by people who routinely were deep wells that watered the souls of those they encountered.

People like Bill are hard to recognize because they are always doing something for God. Think about people in your orbit who you consider a friend and partner in ministry that for whatever reason, might get lost by the local Body of Christ. Perhaps, they are an area Bishop, Director, or Supervisor that as a routine part of the job, is in a different church every Sunday. Maybe it is a volunteer in your church that has gotten overly invested in an outside ministry and you don't see them as much, but assume they are doing fine because they are working so hard for that ministry. It could even be someone who you still think of as connected and vibrant, but if you look closely, it has been a couple of years since they have really had a conversation with you about what God is teaching them, or since you have seen them leaning into their calling.

All of these people, like Bill, not only are burned out, but if you don't intervene (and sometimes even if you do intervene), will flame out. The difference is that the spiritually depleted recognize their condition and just stop, even if it is not a healthy stop. The spiritually defeated stay out front, keep trying to do what they have committed to do, and when they dry up inside, the enemy rains hell on them; before you know it, they have a public failure. The key phrase there is "before you know it." A church with a culture of healing and restoration will learn to recognize those people before that happens. The thinking of people like Bill is that if I don't do it, no one will, so I cannot afford to rest.

Unfortunately, after a Bill flames out, even though they are laity, they have been held in such high esteem, and their flameout is so discouraging to those who trusted and looked up to them, they get treated like pastors who fail. They are ignored, sometimes ostracized, and often criticized. I had many hours of conversation with Bill in the eight months we walked together, and he said to me that many people and pastors said to him, "Let me know if I can help you with anything." I am sure they meant it, but Bill did not know what he needed, and most of those people did not have a plan in place to help him, so nothing concrete was offered and nothing concrete happened.

The Spiritually Mistreated

I do not have time or space here to address all the different ways churches and small groups or individuals in those churches can mistreat people, but let it suffice to say there are toxic people in local churches who can and do mistreat people, leaving them broken and in need of help. It is hard to understand why born again, Spirit-indwelled church members can be so hurtful, but our friends in the counseling profession say that "hurt people hurt people." Maybe they have been wounded themselves and like a wounded animal, lash out at those who are trying to love them. Whatever the reason, these people, left unchecked, can grow toxic and mistreat other believers, leaving them beaten, discouraged, and bitter.

Without getting too far afield from my purpose here, I should also add that when a church gets too many of those kinds of people, the entire church process can become toxic to the point that they do not have a toxic member or group, but the whole church becomes toxic. Think sepsis, but on a spiritual level. Recently, my dear friend, Richard, lost his wife, Diana, to sepsis. What started out minor, strep throat, became toxic because it infected her whole body. By the time she went to the doctor, it had already gotten out of control and they could not rein it in. Unfortunately, there are toxic churches that have the same problem. There were some toxic people that were left unchecked and by the time anyone addressed it, it was too late. The culture became toxic. You can recognize those churches by the number of pastors and staff they call and discard.

You have already heard some of Michael's story. I know there are two sides to every story, but one thing seems pretty clear. Michael and his family were mistreated at the hands of some leaders in the church he was serving. The ministry was expanding, people were coming to Christ, and a community was being impacted, when out of the blue, he was fired, or as we like to say in the Baptist world, "encouraged to resign." By the time I met Mike, he was close to done with ministry and the traditional church. Even worse, his wife and children were so badly mistreated collaterally, that they WERE done with the traditional church. It is the story of a family who has been mistreated and are still living with the results over six years later.

Bryan led a tiny, hurting church through a revitalization process and then agreed to stay on as pastor, growing it from about 25 in attendance to about 100. In the process, he ran afoul of some unwritten rules. Perhaps, you have some unwritten rules in your church. They are easy to run afoul of, because after all, they are UNWRITTEN. They are rules like "check with Bro. Jim before you change the thermostat," or "we like for people to just sit here and worship and give their money for a few years before we let them on a committee."

Bryan is old enough to know better, but he just took them at their word about wanting to reach people and bring some younger people into the church. Of course, he knew those younger people are looking to be involved and find purpose, not just be entertained, so he brought them in and put them to work. As a result, he found himself in deacon meetings month after month, wrestling over every decision. Realizing he was shadow boxing something else, he finally asked them what they wanted him to do and the leader said "resign," so he did. Of course, there is much more to that story, but the bottom line is the same. He and his family were mistreated and even though they came to my church for a while, his family still struggles to fully engage.

Boyd grew up in a strong independent and fundamental Baptist church. He strayed a bit after his parents divorced but found his way back into a small but similar-minded church when he met his future wife. While there, he got active, leading the youth group, teaching, and ultimately declaring his call to ministry. Still a young man, he was hungry for the Word and looking for an opportunity to serve, so he would do anything he could to help.

In an innocent attempt to encourage his pastor, he sent him a link to a sermon he thought might be of use, not noticing the pastor on the podcast was reading from a translation of the Bible not particularly favored by the pastor and the church. Regardless of your feelings about translations, I think we can all agree that if you think that was an error worth addressing, Scriptures would point you toward a private conversation to address the error. Instead, the following Sunday, the pastor called him out publicly during the sermon and in Boyd's words, "berated him for what seemed like an eternity, though it probably was not that long."

It crushed him spiritually and caused him to leave the church. This was difficult for his somewhat introverted wife who had spent her entire life in the church. A chance encounter with a youth pastor at that time brought him to another local church. He is young and resilient and is being used by God in student ministry, and is even pursuing a ministry-related education; but spiritual mistreatment almost derailed him before he got started.

David spent his life in management at one of the largest corporations in Tennessee, and also serving as a bivocational student pastor and later pastor, and serving as a leadership consultant for local churches. He is effusive, gregarious, funny, and talented. After many years of serving the local church on the side, a larger rural church asked him to be their full time pastor. Agreeing to leave his position, his pension, and his accomplishments behind, he settled into the life of a pastor. Soon, he found out there was a cabal of men, some of whom no longer even attended, that made the decisions outside the usual channels and expected the pastor to do what he was told. Again, I know there are two sides to every story, but it is the end of this story that is so discouraging.

He was fired/resigned, whatever you want to call it, and by the time I reconnected with him when I moved back into the area, he had been out of ministry and only on the fringe of church for over five years. Even when he desired to re-engage, his wife was so beat up in the process that she was having none of that. He eventually went on to pastor a small unhealthy church for a few months, but has largely been living quietly behind the scenes for 15 years now. It is another example of the collateral damage that results from churches or its leaders mistreating people.

The Spiritually Retreated

Not everyone that needs restoration had something terrible happen to them or did something terrible to find themselves out of service. Sometimes people just need a place to recoup from a particularly grueling season of life and ministry.

Randall came to us from the pastorate of a small town First Baptist Church in the adjoining state. He drove a LONG way past a lot of churches to get to us. Like many pastors of small churches, he had moved from being a very effective bivocational pastor to taking on a full time pastorate. They treated him well for the most part, and he liked being their pastor. After a grueling season of ministry, he just sensed his work there was over and he needed to recharge for a while before going back at it. He resumed his former secular work and brought his family to our church because someone he worked with invited him and said he would find a safe place there to rest and recoup.

Too often, we assume when we see a former pastor or lay leader not serving in those roles anymore and not using their spiritual gifts, that they have done something to be disqualified or are out of the will of God. That can be true, but it is not always true. When you have been a pastor and you are not a pastor anymore, it is often like living in no man's land. Your pastor friends are not on the same flight path as you anymore, and the people you used to hang around pre-pastorate have moved on. Retreating pastors need a friend while they retreat and encouragement at the right time to get back to the task. Often, they need a pastor and friend who will look for ways to give them outlets to preach, minister, and otherwise use their gifts while not in an official position.

Leaving the 99, to look for the 1

A ministry friend who has his own story of brokenness and restoration preached to me a great message on restoration from Luke 15 over a cup of coffee recently.[2] He reminded me that while we get uber-focused on the prodigal son, there are two other lost items in that chapter. One of those, of course, is the lost sheep. The parable begs the question of a shepherd, if you have 100 sheep and one goes missing, will you not secure the 99 and leave them behind while you pursue the lost sheep? Of course, the answer is yes, but we have tens of thousands of lost sheep scattered across our communities that no one is pursuing.

This pastor said that the first act of restoration for the local church is to pursue the missing church members from their own roll. They, like the missing sheep, are probably bruised and nasty and weak. Like the shepherd of the Bible, it is incumbent upon us as a church and as a leader to put them on our shoulder and bring them back. You can imagine that those wandering sheep were matted with fleas and all kinds of nastiness in their fleece, and so are missing church members; but we are to love them enough to clean them up and return them to the rightful place in the flock.

In addition to your own church members, your community is filled with missing sheep from other flocks that are not going to pursue and restore them. It is pretty easy to discern those kinds of sheep when you hear them talk. Ask them about church and they will say something like "I don't go much anymore, but I used to be really active at a church. I helped drive the van and taught Sunday School." Sometimes a simple follow-up question, like "What happened?" will reveal to you another lost sheep in need of a shepherd to restore them.

---

[2] Used with permission.

To a pastor or church leader, all this sounds like more work for an already overworked and understaffed leadership. Step back a moment, though, and consider the ROI (return on investment). There are gaps to fill in your leadership structure, a shortage of children's workers, no one to drive the van, and let's not even talk about needing help to keep the building maintained. There is never enough help or enough time in a church that is trying to advance the Kingdom.

However, consider that it is not just another task to add to a calendar that already has too many entries. It is an investment in future leadership. It has been my personal experience at my church that people who have tasted the grace of God and received a second chance are some of the kindest, most faithful and compassionate people in the church. They know what it was like for God to use them in big ways, and they know the hollow emptiness of a life where they either do not or are not permitted to use the gifts God placed in them to serve. They have experienced the fulfillment of serving God and then the discontent of not being useful. When they get a second chance, they are more seasoned and mature and focused this time around, and they love to serve.

At the time of this writing, Antioch church is staffed by four of us pastors who have been given another chance. Some of us needed a second chance because we messed up and some of us needed a second chance because we were messed over. The common denominator among the four of us is that we all love what we do and are thankful for an opportunity to be there.

At the same time, our church is filled with people from that demographic we mentioned earlier, the chronically de-churched. When we met them, they were out of church for a long period of time or had recently been through a season of pain related to church. Some were burned out and some had flamed out. Some needed a long process of restoration and some just needed a friend. All needed a place where the culture was one of love, encouragement, and hope! Today, many of those people are working in our small groups, ministering to our children, staffing our ministry teams, and leading us in worship.

Before You Move On

We all know our church needs a specific plan of evangelism and one of discipleship. We know there needs to be a plan in place to grow our people in prayer and Bible reading. Why do we not realize that Jesus was serious about restoration and put a plan in place to develop a culture that is conducive to seeking the lost sheep? Oh, God, give us eyes to see the lost sheep, the ones missing from our church and the ones hiding in our community.

For Further Thought:

1. Take a moment and ask God to give you eyes to see some of the lost sheep from your own congregation that are in need of your pursuit and restoration. Write their names below and begin to pray about timing and opportunity to reach out to them.

2. Consider your congregation for a minute and ask God to show you the spiritually depleted who are still plodding ahead but need a time of refreshing and encouraging before their burnout becomes a flameout. Jot their names here and look for a way to encourage them and open up dialogue about how they are doing spiritually.

3. Is there one or more pastors or staff members you know who have been mistreated by a church and find themselves either defeated in place or having quit? Have you meant to make some time to reach out to them and encourage them,

but it just keeps getting pushed out by other, more imminently demanding tasks? Why not write their names down and pray for them today, and send them a note right now to schedule a coffee or lunch conversation?

Chapter 3

It's the Right Thing to Do, but It Does Have Some Fringe Benefits

I am a big man. All my life I have struggled to lose weight and keep it off. During the season of writing this book, I am trying to live a healthier life, controlled by the Spirit. I have lost a good bit of weight, but have a way to go. Don't get too excited, though, because I have lost a lot of weight in my life. I am like some women in that I have every size of clothes in my closet. (It's ok, you can smile at that. I have owned it and embraced it.) As I struggle to lose this weight, I am keenly aware there are some things I do not want to do. I do not want to be disciplined enough to drink water instead of peach tea. I do not want to walk unless I can be in the mountains or on a trail somewhere; just walking around the neighborhood is not my thing. I do not want to choose a super food salad over hot wings and banana pudding. I do not want to give up soft drinks. Yet, all these things are necessary for a healthier lifestyle.

Similarly, there are things that churches do not like to do. Church discipline is not a particularly fun process for a pastor or leadership, but is occasionally necessary; and we ignore it at the potential of great harm to the body. For some reason, corporate prayer gatherings in church are one of the hardest things to keep going consistently. I have compared it to wrestling the steering wheel of a car with a bad alignment. You have to keep wrestling the wheel to keep the car in the center of your lane. Yet, all of us know that Jesus called His church to be a House of Prayer, and it is necessary if anything of value is going to happen. It doesn't matter what your outreach strategy is, most of us agree that having a strategy is a key task of leadership, and would also agree that keeping it going is a strenuous activity.

I am convinced that the work of restorative ministry is as vital to the life of the local church as any of those things. Aside from the command we discussed in the last chapter for the shepherd to leave the 99 and pursue the one lost sheep, there are significant practical implications for the church that does not have a culture of acceptance and a process in place for restoring the broken, as well as the man or woman who needs that ministry. What is at stake when a church refuses to be a repair shop for broken believers, and what is the payoff when they choose to do so?

The Reputation of Jesus and the Church

Let's face it. The church has an image problem in America. Some of it is the result of a secular culture that wants to neutralize the church's influence and takes stories and statements from a few and extrapolates them across the church at large to demonstrate how mean and unloving we can be. There is much said about the church that we do not deserve. But we are a lot like the politician in Texas who was called by his campaign manager, who said, "You have to get to Austin. They are telling lies about you there and we need to respond." The politician replied, "I can't. I have to go to Dallas. They are telling the truth about me there!" The problem with the image of the church is that some of the things they are saying are true.

My friend David and I were discussing the divisive nature of politics in America today. David is one of the most conservative Christians I know. Truthfully, he might secretly think I am too far to the left, but he is a kind and loving soul so he does not chide me for it. As we talked, he said he had to quit listening to talk radio because the conservative Christians have become angry and mean-spirited. That is not true of everyone, but he is right. We have developed a reputation for meanness in the church. It has become a cliché' among non-believers and believers both to acknowledge that the Christian army is the only army in the world that shoots its own wounded.

If you are reading this, chances are that is not your position and you care deeply about the wounded. Churches and pastors sometimes don't pursue the wandering sheep and restore them, not because we don't care about them, but because we don't have time to do everything; and honestly, since the wounded tend to wander away, they get "out of sight and out of mind." We get busy doing all the other things that a pastor or leader has to do. That is one of many reasons restorative ministry has to be deliberately team-led in the local church or it will fall off the edge of the page in a hurry.

It makes all kinds of sense for a church to invest their time where they can be most productive, and restorative ministry can be tedious and time-consuming without a lot of visible results in the short term. There are easier people to reach and quite honestly, it is more fun and rewarding to hang out with the pretty, the perfect, and the well-put-together. To be sure, everyone needs Jesus. Old school evangelist Bill Stafford said, "Everybody needs Jesus — the big shot, the little shot, and them that oughta be shot!" When we only focus on those who appear to have it all together, we confirm to a suspicious world that "while the church may say that all are welcome, if they knew how messed up I am, I would not be welcome there."

When we love and stand by the person whose reputation in the community has been destroyed, we are telling the world that the love of Christ is real and lasting. I am not saying we wink at sin and let them just keep doing what they have been doing. I am saying that authentic Christian love in the darkest times will not only affect the person being restored, but will elevate the love of Christ and the reputation of the church in the minds of people in your community who have their own brokenness that no one knows about. When they see grace and truth being modeled, they begin to believe that maybe there is hope for them.

I do not believe the church is represented by the mean-spirited men and women who dominate the conversation today in the blogosphere and on talk radio. I am convinced after being around thousands of pastors and hundreds of churches that most pastors and churches are people of grace and want to help. I am convinced if they understand the need and have the resources at hand and a track to run on, they will be people and places of grace. When more of us put that into action, the reputation of the church will be elevated in the eyes of the broken, and in the eyes of those who are lost and far from God.

The Leadership Vacuum

I am not a researcher either by qualification or by inclination, so what I am about to say is more observation and anecdotal than by hard numbers. You can read the numbers in your own denomination's publications. If you have been in ministry for any length of time, you see the number of able and willing pastors and staff members to serve in a local church waning. There is a generation of younger pastors who are focused more on planting a church so they do not have to deal with some of the deeply entrenched traditions and barriers to growth they see in long standing and traditional churches. They are both called to church planting and turned off by processes that they see getting in the way of reaching people. That is a discussion for another day, but it contributes to the difficulty churches have in securing competent leadership these days.

Unfortunately, there is a looming financial crisis in the church as well that means a number of pastors, especially those with young families, are having to leave the pastorate not because of personal failure but because of financial reality. The normative church size in the USA is open to debate, but most people agree that while the mega churches get the media, the vast majority of churches are around 100 people or less in average attendance. There was a day when a church of 100 could afford a full time pastor who lived in their parsonage, a part time music minister, and a secretary. Some even were able to pay a youth pastor/worker. The financial realities of life as we approach the 2020s are vastly different. Churches can't afford to pay a living wage that includes adequate medical coverage, so some young men are having to choose to work a secular job and pastor part time, or just attend church and use their gifts in other ways, just to provide health insurance. I have had coffee in recent weeks with two colleagues who have had to make that decision.

Concurrently, there is a growing disregard and disrespect for the local pastor that discourages people from pursuing it as a career. When I began in ministry, everyone at least knew and identified with a pastor whether they attended church or not. Recently, I was talking to a seasoned church planter in the state of Nevada who said when he introduces himself as a pastor, he might as well have said he is an astronaut. People in that area are as likely to have personally met an astronaut as they are to have met a pastor. Couple that with the news stories and blog attacks on pastors who have either sinned or been accused of sin unjustly. We live in a time that accusation is tantamount to guilt. I understand the calling is more than being about a career, but people that might be willing are not even exploring it, as the church has played into the narrative of the media about pastors.

The combination of the lack of supply of up-and-coming pastors with the exodus of current pastors has already reached the crisis tipping point among some of our denominations, and others are watching it come down the pike like an oncoming train. Even as I write this, Southern Baptists have adopted as a key plank in their Vision 2025 strategy a component to "Increase the total number of workers in the field through a new emphasis on 'calling out the called,' and then preparing those who are called out by the Lord."[3] It is an acknowledgement of the coming dearth of pastors. At the same time, there are hundreds of broken and hurting pastors and former church members scattered across our communities who, with a plan and process and a second chance, will make competent and committed leaders for some of these congregations.

I recognize that we each have a different understanding of what actions can completely and permanently disqualify a minister from ever serving as pastor or in a leadership position again. And yet, we have to acknowledge that if he is a follower of Jesus Christ, has been gifted by the Spirit, and given to the body of Christ, the local church, he should be using those gifts for the glory of God, the expansion of the Kingdom, and the development of the saints. I heard Tom Cheyney pose the question, "What about a dying church brings God glory?" I would pose a different question: "What is there about a broken pastor living in local church exile that brings glory to God?"

Their Spiritual Gifts

I drive old cars — not the cool old cars that make people stop and look, but the kind of old cars that make people point and laugh. Don't feel sorry for me. It is not because my church does not pay me well, nor that I cannot afford a better car. Cars just mean nothing to me; they are simply a mode of transportation to get me from point A to point B. I don't think it is wrong to buy nice cars, I just have no interest in the appearance or brand of my car. I have not made a long term

---

[3] Biblical Recorder Website. https://www.brnow.org/news/floyd-issues-vision-2025-call-to-reach-every-person-with-the-gospel/ Accessed June 18, 2020.

car payment since 1992. The last three cars I have owned were so used up by the time I was finished with them, there was ZERO trade-in value. I just gave them to people who needed transportation to get from home to work and did not need to get too far from home.

What does concern me about my car is that it starts easily and doesn't break down. I see lots of old cars up on blocks or sitting around garages in various states of repair. Those mean nothing to me because they appear to be totally unusable and unprofitable for anything. I keep my cars roadworthy and when they can no longer be trusted to be roadworthy, they are disposed of in some way. It is not a decision I make lightly. I don't give up on my church people easily, I never give up on my family, and I rarely give up on my car.

Currently, I am driving an 18-year-old Ford Explorer with 220,000 miles on it. Recently, it bit the dust and for the first time, I realistically considered putting it out of its misery. I have a trusted mechanic, Steve, who takes care of the old boy. I asked his advice and he was 50-50. I polled some friends like me who drive older cars and asked them if they would rebuild the transmission. Their advice was split pretty evenly down the middle. Remember, I am cheap when it comes to cars. I hate car payments. I like my car. So, I took it to a place that rebuilds transmissions and $1,800 later, I was out the door with a guaranteed promise that the transmission was good for at least 12,000 miles. Now it is useful again. I nearly gave up on it, but I did not; and while its days are numbered, we have had some good miles together since then and I am hopeful for many more.

The church in general and the local church in particular has a bad habit when someone "breaks down." It is a habit of forgetting all the good they have done, all the people they have impacted, and all the good qualities God instilled in them at their new birth. We forget that God did not give them those gifts for their own good, but for the building up of the body of Christ. As a result of this spiritual amnesia, when someone is hurt or has failed, we often are not only comfortable with them leaving the church, we actually prefer it. Consider how that must look to God, who saved them and placed them in that local body. I understand there are circumstances where someone hurts someone or the entire church so badly that restoration in that environment is impossible, but more often than not, especially when it's a lay leader that fails, they are pushed away more in judgment and for our comfort than because it is the will of God.

We forget that while they served, they made a difference because God had uniquely gifted them to fill a ministry role in the church. By sending them into permanent exile, we are not only punishing them, which was never the purpose of church discipline, but we are also punishing the church by tossing aside their giftedness.

When my Explorer refused to pull itself away from the red light that day a few months ago, and in the coming week while I was deciding on restoration or demolition, I cleaned it out, assuming I had driven it for the last time. Don't laugh, but as I got my last stuff out of it and left it behind Steve's shop, thinking in a few days I would sell it for scrap, I patted it on the hood and said thank you for miles of safety and reliability. I even told God thank you for helping me buy the right car to get that many miles, and asked Him to help me find another one so reliable, and I must admit, for a good price.

Then, as I began to think about all the things I love about that car, my mind began to change. I thought about how even on a car that old, the air conditioner still does not leak; that I had put new tires on it recently, and it almost never needs an alignment. I thought about how much I enjoyed the sunroof and driving through the mountains with it open. I remembered all the times I had popped it into four wheel drive and rescued a church member in an occasional mountain area snow storm.

The more I thought about it, the more I decided it was worth investing some money in and saving it for a few more miles. As long as I focused on the dead transmission and the $1,800 it was going to cost, I was willing to trash it. When I began to think of its good qualities, I saw it in a different light.

The problem with broken people is that both for them and for those they let down, the pain and the brokenness is right in their face. They and the people they need most are focused on the event or the earthquake that rocked their relationship, and they completely forget about all the things that are right about that person. They forget all the times he or she was the right person for the right task at the right time, and all the times they blessed and encouraged others. As long as Satan and self can keep you focused on the transgression instead of the person as a whole, restoration will be difficult. But when you begin to step back and take a look at the big picture, you will see they are worth saving.

I Corinthians 12 is one of the places the Scriptures address the need for spiritual gifts in the body of Christ.

14 For the body does not consist of one member but of many. 15 If the foot should say, "Because I am not a hand, I do not belong to the body," that would not make it any less a part of the body. 16 And if the ear should say, "Because I am not an eye, I do not belong to the body," that would not make it any less a part of the body. 17 If the whole body were an eye, where would be the sense of hearing? If the whole body were an ear, where would be the sense of smell? 18 But as it is, God arranged the members in the body, each one of them, as he chose. 19 If all were a single member, where would the body be? 20 As it is, there are many parts,[a] yet one body.

21 The eye cannot say to the hand, "I have no need of you," nor again the head to the feet, "I have no need of you." (emphasis mine)

There is much to say here about spiritual gifts, but take note of the two underlined statements and the truths they speak into restorative ministry. The first simply says the foot can't say that since I cannot be a hand, I am not going to do anything and I am just going to walk away from the body. (See what I did there? "Walk away?")

We will talk extensively in the process section about this, but just let me point out here that restoration is not always about putting a person back in the same church or the same role he or she had before. Often, the broken see the only way back to health and wholeness is to be back in the position they were in before. Jobs change but gifts do not.

There are many circumstances that need to be considered along with God's timing before someone can be back in a position of leadership where they failed. It is not impossible, but it is a challenge. Yet, a deacon who received a DUI charge and has stepped down from his office cannot say to the church that loved him and respected him, "If I can't be a deacon, I won't do anything." In most churches, deacons are set aside to that role because they have the spiritual gift of serving. The broken and messed up member of the body is still a member of the body, and if God wants him to serve without the title of deacon, he needs to do that. His gift is still valid. In fact, at the darkest hour of my life, a pastor in my town who, based on our denominations, would not have been considered an ally, came to see me and spoke Romans 11:29 to me: *"For the gifts and the calling of God are irrevocable."*

The second truth, found in v. 21, says that one member of the body does not have the right to look at another and say "I don't need you." When a church refuses to restore a fallen or broken member, they are essentially saying to that person, "our church does not need you and the gifts you have. We know that our loving Father who desires for our church to be a fully formed body that will do His work in this community

41

looked down and thought we needed you, but we know better than He does and we know that we don't need you."

Churches must understand that the broken and fallen are not lepers, and that their issue is not infectious. They are, in fact, spiritually sick members of the family who will not only benefit from the process of restoration, but will also be a benefit to the church when they are whole and deployed again. There are many churches who do not realize it, but in their zeal to remain a "pure" church, they have thrown away men and women who God never intended to discard. When a church begins to do the hard and often tedious work of restoration, they discover that restored people are a reservoir of gifts that can help the ministry. In most cases, out of gratitude for the church's hand up, they are fiercely loyal and hard workers.

Repair Shop Joy

Let's go back to my broken transmission. Steve, my mechanic, is a general mechanic. He can and does do almost anything. However, rebuilding transmissions is a specialty task that he could do, but it would take so much time and be such a small return on his investment, it makes no sense to do it. He did offer to help me buy a new, crate transmission and replace the old one. He was very honest with me. It would be a lot more money than the rebuild and even that would be an inconvenience to him; but he would do it because he is my friend. If I had pushed him, he would have done it; but he would not have enjoyed it much because it would be out of his normal routine and had great potential to not work out well. It might even damage our professional relationship. A general mechanic shop is just not the place to get a transmission rebuilt.

He sent me to a shop run by a guy I had never met named Bill. Bill was the happiest mechanic I ever met. He

42

had a joke for me every time I went in there, smile lines creased his face, and he was cordial to everyone that came through the door. He never got in a hurry, answered questions, was honest about the possible outcomes, and promised me the wait would be worth the effort.

Steve sending me to Bill is a good analogy for the need for churches to work together in restoration. Antioch Church has evolved into a general restoration shop, so we have worked with both lay persons and clergy, men and women, moral failures and addictions, and much more. We have worked with men who failed their church and men whose churches failed them. We are a small church, though, and cannot do everything. We have also discovered that not every person we meet in need of purposeful restoration is a good fit for our church. There have been times out of compassion I have tried to shoehorn them into our process and they were just not a good fit for our church or staff. Thus, we have learned that we need to have some partners that have specialties in restoration and cultures that are different from ours, that will meet the needs of some of the people we meet.

One of the places that is evident is when someone has either wounded the church so badly, the people cannot get past the pain to see the good they did in the past, or the hurt affected so much of the church population, it is not a safe place to heal for them. Even though I believe with all my heart, every church needs to pursue the one, the pastor and leaders also have a responsibility to protect the innocent sheep among them. A large percentage of the time, when a pastor calls me about his own need or the need of a staff member or layperson from the church, after hearing the circumstances, I advise them to stay actively involved in the restoration process, but it cannot happen in the context of their church.

Remember Bill from an earlier chapter? His wife and daughter were still active at my church and they had heard him repent and apologize insincerely so often, that nothing he or I could have said at that point would have convinced them he was for real. They needed the church more than I needed him attending there. Three of the four members of his restoration team were from Antioch, but he did not come back to Antioch. I have as much responsibility to defend his family as I do to restore him. When I was going through my own fumbling, stumbling restoration process ten years ago, it was best for me to do it at another church. The team was from the church I had been serving, but I was pastored by someone else.

Just like Steve sent me to smiling Bill, the transmission guy, my team sent me to a pastor with a loving heart toward broken people. One of the unexpected fringe benefits of the ministry of restoration for me has been the wonderful friendships, resources, and restoration "specialists" I have met along the way. One of the common denominators of all of them is that they smile about restoring people the same way Bill smiles about restoring transmissions.

Trophies of Grace

It is scary to even consider keeping someone around the church that has caused a problem, embarrassed himself and his family, been divisive, or brought reproach upon the church. There are lots of verses that talk about not putting up with unrepentant sinful believers. Titus was told by Paul to warn a divisive person once and then again, and then have nothing more to do with them. We are not talking about restoring the unrepentant. We are talking about allowing the Holy Spirit to use us to bring conviction, repentance, and healing to a fallen servant. When they are repentant, we are offering them a roadmap back to spiritual wholeness and usefulness, even if it is not in the same role they filled before.

As you can see, two things have to happen. There has to be genuine brokenness and repentance, and there has to be a culture and process of healing and restoration that will get them back on their feet. When those two things intersect, it is a beautiful thing. When a brother or sister who has been set aside from their place of service and has felt the isolation and defeat inflicted upon them by a very real predator (who paces about seeking to devour us) is finally freed up to return to Kingdom usefulness and endorsed and supported by the very people he offended, God is glorified. Again I ask, "What about a broken or fallen brother or sister living in isolation and defeat brings glory to God?" Nothing! Restoration brings glory to God.

When a pastor and a church begin to celebrate the day the one who has been reclaimed is returned to the flock in good health and continues to fulfill his or her role in the group, the secretly broken begin to believe they can be honest about their sin and their pain. When the wounded from other churches who are not forgiving and restoring hear that this church is a place where it is ok not to be perfect and pretty and well-put-together, they are drawn there. They often just dip a toe in it, because it sounds too good to be true. When they find out it is real, it begins to snowball. There is a deep well of broken and hurting people just waiting to see a place where there is real hope for the broken.

Trusting Hearts

One of the unexpected fringe benefits of restorative ministry is that as broken people are healed, especially when they see it happening right in front of them, those who are cynical about pastors and leaders begin to see people for who they really are. When a leader has offended the church and is discarded, the enemy accuses them in the minds of those they once served, slowly but surely blinding them to the memories of all the good things that leader had done for them and with them. When that happens a couple of times, the enemy then begins to tempt them to think that all pastors and leaders are villains and cannot be trusted.

When a church works hard to love the broken and falling and give them a hand up, and especially when the fallen and broken are restored to meaningful use in the body of Christ, there is evidence of God's redemptive power. It is a reminder to followers that God gives gifts of leadership to the local church and they can be trusted and should be followed (Ephesians 4:11). Those restored become trophies of grace not only in God's eyes, but in the eyes of the congregation. At Antioch, even though they do not always know all the details, members are righteously proud of what God has done through them and genuinely love those who have been restored.

Occasionally, I will be talking to someone I met in the community and inviting them to church and they will ask to meet with me. Over coffee, they lower their voice and whisper about some past sin or fault in their lives. I listen politely and then ask them questions about how they had served in the past and what they have done since the "event." Then, I laugh and tell them some of the stories of our team and say something like, "If you came here to church, you would not even be the worst guy on the stage. You will fit right in." We love our trophies of God's grace.

Before You Move On

Some things you just do because they are the right thing to do. Restorative ministry falls under that heading. It is difficult, doesn't work a significant percentage of the time, and will be viewed with suspicion by church members and skepticism by the broken. If it was easy, everyone would be doing it. But I hope you have seen in this chapter that it is not only worth it to the person who needs help, but is worth it to the church and pastor willing to help.

For Further Thought:

1. Do you know of leadership needs in your church, either staff or laity, that might benefit from a process of restoration? Have you seen the impact losing a key leader to brokenness and failure has had on the ministry you serve?

2. What are some of the gifts of the Spirit that are conspicuously missing in your own church? Begin to ask God who in your community could meet those needs if you were willing to take the time to restore them? (Don't forget — it is not enough to just give them another chance if you are not willing to walk in a process with them.)

3. Are there people in your congregation or community who you can identify that have a difficult time trusting because of failures of former leaders?

Chapter 4

Restoration Theology

The largest earthquake ever recorded with modern seismographic equipment took place on May 22, 1960, near Valdivia, in southern Chile. It was assigned a magnitude of 9.5 by the United States Geological Survey (USGS). It is commonly referred to as the "Great Chilean Earthquake." The earthquake occurred along a fault line beneath the Pacific Ocean off the coast of Chile. The subsequent ground motion and tsunamis left almost three million people across the pacific homeless, and took lives all the way in Hawaii, Japan, and the Philippines.[4]

Fault lines exist under the surface of the earth where a breakage or fault has occurred, causing the rock plates to shift and slide. We call this sliding of underground rock plates an earthquake. Often, there are warnings before an earthquake occurs. Smaller foreshocks shake things up and warn residents that something worse could happen soon. Sometimes there are no warning tremors. Sometimes the warnings are too small to detect, except by using special devices.

Galatians chapter six deals with the rumblings and tumblings of relational earthquakes within the church. The Holman Christian Standard Bible renders the phrase in Galatians 6:1 as, "overtaken in any wrongdoing," meaning that something undetected led to a lapse, or unforeseen mistake. The word "wrongdoing" refers not to willful sin, but to a lapse that left an opening. A fault that led to a larger

---

[4] "World's Largest Recorded Earthquake," Geology.com website. Accessed June 18, 2020. https://geology.com/records/largest-earthquake/.

quake. Something unseen or undetected that led to a visible upheaval.

It is against this background that the Apostle Paul commands those who are spiritually mature to "restore" those overtaken by wrongdoing. This verse (actually, all of Galatians 6:1-10) is the basis for restoration theology, and the process by which those who fall are to be restored to wholeness and usefulness again by the church.

The Baffling Confusion Surrounding Restoration

Although this passage of Scripture has been preached, taught, expounded, dissected, and written about by some of Christianity's most prolific scholars and preachers, confusion still exists within churches and across denominations concerning its application. Too often, the debate hangs up on which sins are "forgivable" and who is "restorable." Church leaders and members are too quick to skip to Galatians 6:7 and self-righteously proclaim that sowing leads to reaping. They fail to acknowledge that verse seven speaks to the spiritually mature of sowing the Spirit, or fruit of the Spirit, among the broken (the entire tone of verses one through eight).

Indeed, most believers across denominational lines have heard the cliché that the Christian Army is the only army in the world that shoots its own wounded. And this from the followers of Him who claimed, "He will not break a bruised reed, and He will not put out a smoldering wick…" (Matthew 12:20 HCSB).

I (Michael) recently worked with a client who invested decades of exceptional service with a Christian university, only to be falsely accused and maligned by the very people he had served. Then the national Christian press jumped onboard the "kick-him-when-he's-down" train without first ascertaining the facts. Therefore, the false narrative perpetuated against him, which has been unequivocally proven to be untrue, was believed and accepted as truth. This servant of Christ, who had spoken and represented this university all over the United States, heard nothing but crickets chirping from his alleged brothers and sisters in Christ.

The Basic Support for Restoration

As Paul addresses the legalistically-leaning Galatian church in chapter six, his focus is to turn them from harsh law to restorative grace. Whoever among them that became overtaken by wrongdoing, overcome by hidden faults that caused surface damage, was to be "restored." The word here means to set a broken bone or mend a broken net. The emphasis is on returning what has become broken to health and usefulness. That is always to be the goal of restoration.

Bearing Burdens

These instructions for restoration contain one of the most baffling portions of Scripture, and a favorite of those who search for "contradictions" in the words of Jesus. Galatians six, verses two and five, feature different words for what is often translated as "burden" or "load."

"Carry one another's burdens; in this way you will fulfill the law of Christ" (vs. 2).

"For each person will have to carry his own load" (vs. 5) HCSB

The two burdens are not contradictory, but complementary. The first burden describes a heavy load. It is something huge that no person can possibly carry alone. Paul may have had Jesus' words from Matthew 23:4 in mind here, where Jesus accused the Pharisees of imposing legal (OT

Law) burdens on the people that no one could carry, or fulfill.

These are burdens like:

- Burden of sin
- Burden of broken relationships with others
- Burden of a broken relationship with God / the church
- Burden of public shame
- Burden of consequences / results of mistreatment

Those who willingly help a fallen brother or sister bear these burdens are said to fulfill (keep, accomplish, obey, perform) the "Law of Christ." Christ's law is one of sacrificial love that fulfills the entire Old Testament Law and the teachings of the Prophets (Galatians 5:14).

The second load or burden in verse five is a word often used to describe a soldier's backpack, which contained his supplies and weaponry required for service. These were personal things used daily that not only made the soldier useful, but enabled him to save lives. I believe this describes the acts of faith and personal discipleship that we can only do for ourselves, such as salvation, prayer, bible study, and faithful obedience. We will only be able to help the fallen carry their unbearable loads as we faithfully meet our own requirements for discipleship.

This is why Paul issues the command of restoration to "you who are spiritual" (vs. 1), meaning those who by carrying out the responsibilities of personal discipleship are equipped to render assistance to others, all the while "watching out for yourselves so you won't be tempted also."

Sowing the Spiritual

Those who engage in the heavy work of restoration demonstrate the humility of Christ Himself (vs. 3-4) that doesn't bother to compare with others, but only focuses on the path laid before them. In this way, they avoid the temptation that caused those needing restoration to stumble. It is in this context that the well-known concept of sowing and reaping is introduced. The example is first given that those who are taught should sow (give, invest, support) the work of those who teach (lead, preach, disciple) others (vs. 6). And it must be said here that a vital part of that support should be bearing the burdens of restoration when a leader stumbles or is caused to fall.

What we invest, we will surely harvest (vs. 7), especially when our investments are of a spiritual nature. Remember that this teaching is within the overall theme of restoration. Paul's message here is to be relentless in our pursuit of personal spiritual disciplines in order to invest spiritual capital in Kingdom work. And a crucial aspect of that work is restoring the broken to health and usefulness for Christ's Kingdom.

Hence, Paul's closing of this section by encouraging us to invest spiritual capital at every opportunity, but especially to brothers and sisters in Christ.

"Therefore, as we have opportunity, we must work for the good of all, especially for those who belong to the household of faith." Galatians 6:10 (HCSB)

A Biblical Snapshot of Restoration

Perhaps the greatest example of biblical restoration in Scripture stems from Peter's adamant denial of Christ before His crucifixion. At first glance, we are amazed that Peter, of all the disciples, would deny that he knew or followed Jesus. This is the same Peter who resorted to violence to prevent Jesus' capture in John 18:10. This is the bold disciple who brazenly declared, "Though they all fall away because of you,

I will never fall away" (Matthew 26:33 ESV). And even, "I will lay down my life for you" (John 13:37 ESV).

But somewhere beneath the surface, a hidden fault, of which Peter was likely unaware, caused a tumultuous public reversal at the worst possible time. Did Peter know a hidden fault line existed in his character? Could he have known that too much pressure at just the right moment would cause him to slide away? Obviously, Jesus knew of this hidden fault; thus His sad prediction in Matthew 26:34. And strong, resilient Peter shamefully and publicly fulfilled Jesus' words in Luke 22:56-60 by denying that he even knew Jesus, much less followed Him.

That chapter closes with Peter bitterly weeping in shame. And, then this once-stalwart follower of Jesus is noticeably absent through the crucifixion narratives. Fast forward to the empty tomb and see Peter marveling in awe and confusion at what has happened to Jesus' body. Peter seems to be with the other disciples, but the brash, bold follower is now silent. He is no longer a leader among them. The loudest has now sunk the lowest.

But in Mark 16:7, the young man in a white robe outside the tomb tells the women there, "But go, tell His disciples and Peter..." *And Peter...* And Peter! Was Peter one of the disciples to whom the young man referred? Yes. But his message was to single Peter out from the rest, to make sure that Peter heard that Jesus desired his company. After a painful and public denial that left Peter weeping and wandering in confusion, Jesus sought to restore him; especially him.

I (Michael) feel Peter's pain as he experiences the post-resurrection appearances of Jesus with the other disciples, and yet is himself still broken and discouraged. In John 21, Peter returns to the only thing that seems solid in his life — his past as a fisherman. He, James, and John return to the familiar, to what might give them a sense of stability again. Perhaps remembering past successes, a feeling of the familiar, something they felt they could control seemed more prudent after everything that had happened when they followed Jesus.

All too often, going backward onto familiar ground gives the broken a sense of stability. I know that it did for me. Returning home to the house in which I grew up, surrounded by family and a familiar setting, felt safe. It was not the ideal, in many ways. But it was something solid I felt I could land on when the bottom fell out of my life and ministry.

But Jesus wasn't finished with them yet, and especially not with Peter. John 21 continues with Jesus making a special effort to forgive Peter and restore him to usefulness. Jesus models for us what Paul later instructs the church to do in Galatians 6 — restore the broken to health and usefulness.

The Backlash Suffered from Restoration

Sadly, the work of biblical restoration is too often misunderstood, neglected, or completely ignored. As we have demonstrated (and as you will see reiterated throughout this book in the stories it contains), our world is filled with broken, hurting, and all-but-forgotten members of the Body of Christ who desperately needed restoration and did not receive it.

Confused Churches

Within local churches of every stripe, there is a palpable tension of denominational and church traditions regarding whether or not a person can ever be useful for ministry again in the church where they failed, or even in another church. Opinions differ about which sins are restorable and which are not. Well-meaning church members ask questions like:

- Should a local church body allow a fallen minister or church member into their fellowship for care and restoration, or should such people be held at arm's length?
- Are there not "special programs or places" for such people, to keep them from soiling the reputation of a local church?
- Won't it hurt our church's testimony and witness if it becomes known we are "harboring sinners" or "condoning sin?"
- Shouldn't this be a ministry only for larger churches with the resources to handle it and keep it hidden from public (or church) knowledge?

Moreover, a church that makes a concerted effort at biblical restoration will often take a hit, their reputation being trampled by others who don't share the same beliefs. They become known as "that church," the one that lowers its standards just to attract people.

Prideful People

Within the church are those people who are more concerned with what others think than with obedience to Christ's teachings. A friend and mentor of mine (Michael) from my days at Mid-America Baptist Theological Seminary impacted me greatly. Years after my days as a student, my friend became injured and began a long and painful recovery. During his recovery, he became addicted to the pain medications his doctors prescribed as part of his recovery. Even after his shoulder injury had healed, he still craved and obtained the medication. When my friend found himself pawing through a parishioner's medicine cabinet while making a visit, he knew that he needed help.

My friend brought his condition and needs to the attention of his church's governing body, confessed his addiction and subsequent wrongdoing, and asked for help.

55

Thankfully, this church responded with grace and compassion, and helped him find the help he needed to overcome this addiction.

After leaving this church to serve another as senior pastor, my friend's old addiction reared its ugly head again. This new church reacted differently to my friend's needs. After initially agreeing to provide the help he needed, they reversed themselves and decided not to provide any assistance whatsoever. My friend resigned from the pastorate and left the church.

As if that were not enough, as he sought help on his own, my friend chose another church to attend on the far side of the county from the church that had refused to help him. On that first Sunday morning, the pastor, who knew my friend from the previous church, welcomed him and invited him out for coffee later that week. But at that coffee meeting, the pastor informed my friend that his church leadership had asked the pastor to let him know that he was not welcome at their church. They were aware of what happened at my friend's recent pastorate, and they did not want his reputation soiling their own. My friend moved out of state to be near a support network of family and is currently out of ministry.

Pride is a reprehensible sin that finds its root in rebellion, an attitude that God compared to witchcraft (1 Samuel 15:23). People who consider themselves above the sins committed by others, or who see themselves as beyond the temptation to sin, are poison to the restorative ministry of the local church.

Discouraged Denominational Leaders

All too often, area Mission Directors or other denominational leaders are caught in the middle when a church upheaval occurs and a minister is forced to leave. A pastor or staff member falls or is forced out, and the church moves on searching for a replacement. The area denominational leader's role is to work with area churches to help them grow and be healthy, and that includes preparing to call new leadership or staff. At the same time, he or she undoubtedly wants to aid the former church leader. In most cases, the denominational leader doesn't have the knowledge or resources to provide what the former church leader needs, and must walk a tightrope. On one side is being a friend to the hurting, while on the other side is maintaining relationships with the troubled church, and other area churches and leaders, many of whom harbor their own opinions about what happened and can make their opinions known, putting added pressure on the denominational leader.

I (Michael) experienced this dichotomy when my former church asked me to leave and covered it up. A local denominational leader was and is a great friend, but he was literally powerless to help me in any way, and still had to maintain a good relationship with the church, which wields significant influence in his area. He was vocal in his opposition to their actions, but ministry to the churches must continue whether the denominational leader wants to or not.

This kind of quagmire also leaves landmines behind for when the denominational leader must deal with the pastor who comes behind the ousted leader. The area leader knows the truth about why the former pastor left, but how much has the incoming pastor been told by the church? And how much of what has been told is accurate? How much can/should the denominational leader share? While complete honesty should always be our default, what if that honesty jeopardizes the denominational leader's position, and by extension, his livelihood?

These situations leave local denominational leaders discouraged at the actions of churches under their care, and at their inability to provide help. The ousted minister often leaves the area, making it difficult or impossible to provide he or she any assistance. And the church in question pridefully refuses any attempt by the denominational leader to point out its mistakes. One local denominational leader told me, concerning ministers and churches that failed in their relationship, that he had never seen a situation where both parties did not make dumb mistakes. And this typically leaves the denominational leader's hands tied.

Counting the Cost

For the servant of Christ and the local church that chooses to engage in restoration ministry, a warning is in order. Elsewhere in this book my co-author (Pete) has voiced the same admonition: restoration ministry is hard work, and there will be opposition. Not everyone in your church, your circle of friends, or even your family will understand or be sympathetic. Many will be verbal in their opposition, and many will go further, seeking to impede the mission at every opportunity.

It is imperative that churches and ministers agree to cultivate the necessary culture of humility and grace before attempting serious efforts at restoration. It will be difficult enough for many churches to simply allow a broken minister and his or her family to attend their church. Part of cultivating the necessary church culture includes counting the cost and being willing to suffer reproach. But fear not —you are in good company.

"So also Jesus suffered and died outside the city gates to make his people holy by means of his own blood. So let us go out to him, outside the camp, and bear the disgrace he bore. For this world is not our permanent home; we are looking forward to a home yet to come."
Hebrews 13:12-14 (NLT)

Before You Move On

This is a crossroads moment in which you have to decide whether you move forward in restoration ministry or you decide the cost is too high. Take a few minutes to reflect and pray on the following questions.

For Further Thought:

1. Evaluate your own restoration theology. Do you believe there are sins beyond restoration? What are they?

2. What are the personal, church, and denominational constructs in your experience about restorative ministry and broken people that have formed your restoration theology? Are they all Biblical or are some of them based on tradition?

3. Realistically, from your current view and perspective, what are the potential practical costs to you and your church for choosing to be a restoring congregation?

Chapter 5

Who Needs It?

I am deeply indebted to my friend David, who practices restoration in a full time ministry on a scale that most of us reading this book will never have the time to do. All of us work somewhere in the tension between our own faults and failures and our public reputation, and David is no different. He knows what it is like to be broken, and he knows like no one else I have ever met what it means to have his enemies attack him relentlessly and viciously because of his failures. The attacks seem rooted in his audacity to think God can use him again, and horrors, might even use his brokenness to help someone else in their moment of need. It looks to me a lot like Romans 8:28 and that God is using David's "all things" to work good in both his life and the lives of hurting people, and that he is fulfilling his purpose in this stage of his life.

I have been teaching and ministering to people in my community for the last several years on a micro scale compared to what I see exhibited in David's life and ministry. That is, restoration is not just helping pastors who have had an affair get back in ministry. In fact, that is neither the focus nor the goal. We will discuss in the next chapter what restoration is and is not, but before we do, consider when an intervention is called for and when you need to step in and offer to walk in the difficult valley with someone.

In the writing of this book, I spent a few days with David, watching his counseling and interaction, and talking to him about dozens of different people they have hosted, counseled, encouraged, and connected to others who could help them. He and his wife are like air traffic control for those in need of restoration. They deal with pastor's wives who have been wounded and comfort pastor's wives who have been widowed. They take in pastors who have been fired both justly and unjustly. They love on the families affected by family members who are same-sex attracted. David carries on correspondence with men in jail who were former pastors, lay leaders, and staff members. Their days are filled with phone calls, personal visits, and letter writing. I was overwhelmed by the variety of needs in the ministry of restoration. In my local church, I always have one or more people who fall in that group, but to face them all at one time would overwhelm me. I am thankful for people like David.

The takeaway from my time with him and his wife is that restorative ministry is a variety of needs being met in a variety of ways by a variety of people. Most of us in our local churches will never deal with some of the things people like David face; at least not on that scale. We will face over the course of time, though, many different needs, and we have to know up front there is no cookie cutter, one-size-fits-all program or process for restoring a fallen or broken believer. The following is by no means an exhaustive list of the ways you can encounter brokenness and the needs you will address, but before we go on, we need to at least consider some of the different ways the enemy of our soul breaks and overtakes our people. Each of these situations will require a different level of commitment on your part, will necessitate a different support team, and demand a different level of commitment from the person you are dealing with.

Pastors

A major reason pastors and churches have not embraced the idea of restorative ministry is that we get fixated on those pastors who have made big mistakes and committed big sins, and we think restoration is about giving them a pass. We do not recognize the variety of needs among pastors and see the incredible opportunity God has given us to rescue his wounded soldiers. We also have a mistaken notion that restoration is about just putting people back to work. Consider some of these pastors you may know.

Pastors Whose Sins Have Gone Public

All of us are sinners both by nature and by choice, so it is hard to talk about pastors who sin without sounding like pastors are supposed to be above sin. However, there are some sins that clearly disqualify a pastor from serving any longer in the position they were in when the offense occurred. Depending on your tradition and faith group, your opinion of whether or not that is a permanent disqualification may be different, but the pastor who breaks his marriage vows or falls into some other vice that is clearly contrary to his employment contract is in need of restoration.

His life has come to a screeching halt. His identity as a pastor has been wrested from him. He has lost the respect and the friendship of many or all of his colleagues. He needs a friend who knows the path forward. It may have been years since he had a pastor of his own, but he needs one now.

Pastors Who Have Been Accused

In the era of #metoo, accusation is the same thing as guilt in the minds of many, and portions of the church have adopted this philosophy as well. When one has been accused of something they actually did and will not confess (in appropriate circles) and repent, there can be no restoration. The hard truth here, though, is that if someone has been wrongly accused, many will believe it, and he is going to need someone to stand with him, believe in him, and give him a way to move forward.

Reputations are hard to reclaim and restoration in that situation is often found in just being willing to be identified with the accused. There is a man I have known for many years whose failure was published in the newspaper and broadcast far and wide. But the accusations were blown up. He sinned and he freely admitted it, resigning from a large church and leaving ministry altogether for several years. He was *not* guilty, however, of what he was accused of publicly. In fact, the charges were dropped and the one who accused him was charged with a crime for accusing him. He put himself in a position to be accused and suffered horrible consequences. Now, after many years of rebuilding his marriage and family, he is back to pastoring a small church near my boyhood home. I attend meetings with him from time to time and watch as he sits alone. I try to make sure he doesn't, because a brother who has been accused needs a friend to sit with him.

Pastors Who Have Been Fired

Pastors are not always fired because of sin. They can lose their jobs because they are incompetent in one or more areas, because they accidentally killed the sacred cow, because they do not live up to the standards of the idolized former pastors, or just because they rubbed the power brokers the wrong way. Perhaps we think it is "catching" and are afraid to be seen with those hurting colleagues. Maybe we just get busy and don't think about them. We mean to reach out to them, but because it is not part of our routine, it slips away from us. Whatever the reason, we fail them.

There are ways the church can restore them while benefiting from their experience. They need to be loved and accepted after being told by another church they are unacceptable. We can give them small responsibilities in areas where they were deemed lacking and help them hone the necessary skills. We can give them a platform to use their desire to teach. We can even give them a role, either paid or unpaid, on our staff, since it is always easier to get a job when you already have a job. The first step back is always the hardest, and if they can say to a prospective church that they are serving as minister of something at your church, you have helped them immensely while gaining some valuable help and experience while they are with you.

Pastors and Families Wounded by the Church They Still Serve

I remember a young wife and mother sitting in our living room with her husband a few years ago. They were leading a vibrant ministry in an old, established church. Most churches would have loved them and been thankful for the kind of success they were having. Because of their success, they were in no danger of being fired. In fact, they stayed on in that church for several more years. Here she was, though, pouring her heart out to us about ways people had hurt them and had communicated to them that they were not "one of us" and would never be truly accepted. Through tear-filled eyes she said, "They just don't love us."

Among your colleagues in ministry are some who are in a tough place to serve, but they know this is God's assignment and they cannot leave. They communicate that from time to time with a veiled prayer request or a preacher joke about their leadership structure. I know anytime preachers get together, there is a little bit of whining going on, but this is deeper than that. You will miss it if you don't slow down and make eye contact. Even if they are not in your church, there are things you can do to bind up the brokenhearted and lift up the feeble. You won't do it, though, if you don't see them — really see them.

Pastors That Are Depressed or Anxious

Philippians 4:6 clearly tells us not to be anxious, but thankfully, churches don't typically see anxiety or depression as a fireable offense. It is not something we want our pastors talking about, especially publicly. Dale Wolery of the Clergy Recovery Network and Dale Ryan of Christian Recovery International wrote "Putting our best foot forward can easily mean putting our struggles out of sight. (Members) may not want, for example, to invite visitors on Sunday and then find that the pastor has decided to talk about his struggles with depression during the sermon. Who, we think, will be attracted to our church if our pastor is depressed? If the pastor can't be truly happy, who can be?"[5]

Pastors whose church needs them to pretend perfection are sitting ducks for the enemy to attack and take them down. If they cannot be honest with the church they serve, they desperately need a place and a friend where they can be honest. Restoration may mean providing resources such as counseling, retreat locations, or just being their friend. Pay attention to your colleagues and notice changes of demeanor that settle in for a long time. All of us in the helping professions have emotions of depression and anxiety that are tied to circumstances, but when the emotion of depression becomes a spirit of depression, someone needs to step in.

Church Members

Again, we think of spiritual restoration as being only the process of helping a fallen vocational minister get back to using his skills and gifts in a local congregation, but it is so much more than that. When Paul wrote to his friends in Galatians 6:1, he was not talking to a professional clergy, but about brothers and sisters in the church who were running the race well and got overtaken from behind by a fault they may not have even realized they had. We have a habit of assuming that when a layperson falls away or commits a huge

---

[5] "Beating the Pedestal Syndrome," NACR website. Accessed June 18, 2020. https://www.nacr.org/resource-center-on-emotional-and-relational-health/beating-the-pedestal-syndrome-help-for-pastors-drowning-in-the-ministry.

blunder, they are simply rebellious. Far too often, they are so busy helping around the church that the fault sneaks up on them. Some are more susceptible than others because they have things in their past that have not been dealt with, and a simple process of purposeful restoration would make a difference.

Members Who Have Suffered Clergy Abuse

In today's climate of sexual abuse and the revelation of old crimes, when we say clergy abuse, what pops into our head is a pastor molesting a child. That does happen and that is happening, although I hope the awareness of late has eliminated some of it. When I talk about clergy abuse, I am not talking about that. You may need to minister to the person or family who was abused in that way, but most of that work should be left to the professionals.

What I am talking about here is clergy who abuse their power and position for personal gain or to get their way. It might happen without malice by the pastor who thinks he is right and the end justifies the means, but your community is populated with people who either quit church or faded into the background because of mistreatment by a pastor. They are going to need a season of restoration to get back on their feet. For a deeper understanding of this, David Johnson and Jeff VanVonderen's book, *The Subtle Power of Spiritual Abuse*, is a good place to start.

Members Whose Sins Have Become Public

Like pastors, church members sometimes commit sins that become public, and are such that they have to give up any position of leadership or influence they have in the church. The problem when it happens to a church member rather than a pastor is two-fold. The member likely has deep roots in the church and no prospect of being called to a different church at some point, as most pastors at least can hope to occur. They also have a professional life outside the church; that means they have something to run toward that pastors often do not. These things make it far more likely they will just leave the church altogether, and far less likely they will engage in a process of restoration and healing.

Like pastors, there are some sins that would make it very difficult for that member to stay in your church, so it behooves us to have resources and a network so we can at least try to hand them off. Additionally, from time to time, someone who has had a problem in another church will begin attending your church. This can occur either without them disclosing why they left their former church, or if they do disclose what happened, without going through any process to build a foundation that won't let it happen again. You have a responsibility to have a plan and process in place for those who want it, and a responsibility to protect your flock from those who are unrepentant and don't want restoration, but *do* want a return to prestige and position.

Members Who Have Been in or Caused a Church Fight

I know, I know; you are thinking, "Surely, churches do not get into fights." While I am sure you never experienced or heard of such a thing, it is sadly true. My invalid mother sits in her chair for hours at a time watching her hummingbirds fight over the feeders. There are always more feeders than hummers, but they want what the other one has, much like people.

It is a good illustration of church members who have all they need in Christ but try to fight others and run them off from the never ending source. I don't get it. Yet, there are people who live in your community and some who have begun to attend your church that have been in those fights.

Do your homework. Just because they have been in a fight does not mean you don't want them. But people who have been in a fight are wounded and more easily susceptible to being used in church conflict.

I was working with a church in a consulting role that had recently been through a split that brought their numbers down so low, they were considering disbanding. Ground zero for the last split was a deacon chairman who had been in the church for just a couple of years when they made him a deacon. By the time I was involved, he had moved on, but there was a lot of scorched earth as a result of his leadership. When working through the process with the church and meeting with him to hear his story, I discovered that he had been wounded in one church fight; moved to another church where he was a deacon and chairman during a church fight that resulted in him leading a walkout during a church business meeting; and then wound up at this little church where he was involved in a third split. After meeting with him, I was not convinced he was a bad guy or looking for a fight, but having been wounded and never working through it, he was an easy target of a wily enemy. He would have benefited greatly from the investment of a church and a process before he was put back in leadership, and this hurting church would have been spared the death blow.

There are as many ways people can need restoration as there are ideas in the mind of Satan who wants to steal God's gifts from the local church, kill His leaders and His work, and destroy the good works that have already been done. My hope is that this will get you thinking about the deep well of need AND the untapped resources who are living on the fringes of your church family and in the community where you live.

Cain gave in to sin and killed his own brother out of pride and hurt feelings, not at Abel, but at God. When confronted with his sin by God, he indignantly asked, "Am I my brother's keeper?" Some of you are reading this and have this sense that you need to do something. Or you may have a friend who has stumbled and you feel an obligation to them. But deep inside, there is a little bit of Cain in you. You have the fleeting thought that he or she should have been stronger, sought help, or resisted temptation. You might even think, "I am tending to my own issues; can't they?" Something inside you whispers, "Am I my brother's keeper?" Down through the corridors of time, God has always answered "yes" to that question. You are your brother's keeper, and restoration is part of the job description!

For the pastor who would foster a culture of restoration in his church, it requires a spirit that is willing to confront but not be mean spirited and superior. Arrogance is the silent killer behind most sins of leaders, and is the result of a life lived on a pedestal with no accountability.

Before You Move On

For the church leaders who see the need and have a desire to foster a culture of restoration in their congregation, and who see the need for a process of restoration, it requires a unique combination of abilities and willingness that often seem like they don't go together. Restorers must have the heart of a champion that is willing to confront hurting people with truth they may not want to hear. I am hesitant to use the word 'confront,' because often those who confront do so in a mean spirited way that comes across judgmental, even when it is not intended that way. It requires a soft answer that will turn away wrath while being firm. The difficult truth is that you cannot help someone if they do not want you to help them, so you must be firm but kind. You also cannot help them when they are desperate for help and you appear to be self-righteous. Proverbs 27:6 reminds us that "faithful are the wounds of a friend." They still hurt; but delivered in the kindness of genuine empathy and friendship, they are palatable and can be understood as for one's own good. Wounds that do not come from a friend are not faithful and accomplish nothing.

Certainly, you have to take off the rose-colored glasses and see the situation for what it really is, but it is equally important as a friend that you don't allow that broken, hurting believer to get fixated on the failure alone. You can't forget, and you can't let them forget, that God has used them in some important ways, and the event that brought them to this place is not the sum of their life's work. Being a friend means telling the truth both about the problem, but also about the value of their service to the Kingdom of God.

For Further Thought:

1. What is the track record of your congregation as it concerns either laity or clergy who have sinned or broken trust in some way? Where are those people now? Did the church do anything to help them move forward from that event or connect them with resources that could help them? Did you do all that was in your power alone to help them find restoration?

2. Has this chapter helped you to see some people in a new light? Are there those in your circle of influence that you have seen as perhaps lazy or unspiritual that you now realize may be wounded or broken?

3. What are some resources, both people in your congregation and connections you have outside of your people, that you can identify as a potential partner in restoration?

Chapter 6

Restoration is and Is NOT

Restoration is not about making things like they used to be, even in personal relationships. Restoration instead is a process by which bridges can be built between the broken/failed leader or member and his significant relationships that have been adversely affected by the event or problem. It is about building bridges between a defeated brother or sister and the loving heavenly Father that they may feel they have let down. Depending on their theology, they may feel God is mad at them or punishing them. It is about building bridges between the restoree's past and his or her future usefulness to the Kingdom.

Restoration offers a safe venue where sins can be revealed, acknowledged, and repented from, and sincere apologies and amends can be made at the appropriate time. Most 12-step programs include step 8 which says, "Make a list of all persons we have harmed and become willing to make amends to them all;" followed by step 9, "Make direct amends to such people, wherever possible, except when to do so would injure them or others."

By now you may have taken time to visit my (Pete) website to hear and read more of my story. I won't write the whole story in these pages, but it came to a head one week in July of 2008. My depression and anxiety had certainly morphed from a season into a spirit that hovered about me. I quit sleeping almost completely and was walking around in a fog that never lifted. With my wife's help, I would pull myself together and get out the door for required events, but just doing daily life was getting to be a chore. By that time, I knew I was in trouble, but in my pride and self-reliance, mushed on in my own power.

The final week included several events that I am not proud of, including an altercation with our executive pastor at a church picnic; a yelling match in a staff meeting; and finally a night where I considered suicide, alcohol, drugs, or anything else to numb the pain.

For some of you, you might put this book down when you read the next statement. It is raw, but it is true. I was driving down the road toward an unexpected hospital visit with my sunroof open and screaming heavenward at God, asking why He was doing this to me. After all, I thought having served Him all my life, it was not fair that this was happening to me. It makes no sense now and it should not have then, but it was the way I felt.

Throughout that evening, God gave me several opportunities to turn around and seek help, but I refused each one. There was a text from a woman who prayed for me but had never texted me. I didn't even recognize the number. As I left the hospital, I stood in the hallway for 30 minutes considering and debating whether I should go to the ER or not. Several more times, I had doors of escape opened to me.

Later, in the restoration process, I would be asked what red lights I had run on the way to this event. It was both profound and ironic, as at one point that night, I sat through two cycles at a red light until someone blew their horn at me. I was trying to decide whether to go home and ask for a leave of absence or not. I would later find out that person was an undercover policeman, and that encounter attracted his attention, so he decided to keep his eyes on me.

He followed me down the road until in a moment of lucidity, I decided to make a U-turn and go home. When I made that turn suddenly and without a signal, he shot by me. I did not know that he was coming back or that he was even there. He thought I was trying to evade him, apparently, based on a conversation we would have within minutes.

When I made that sharp turn, I had the windows down and heard someone yell. I thought I had hit someone and stopped. A lady got in the car and asked me for a ride. In my right mind, I would have parked the car and got out right there and left. She was in my car no more than a minute, but as I pulled away, the policeman had made a U-turn himself and pulled in behind me and turned on his lights. Turns out he had been following me for a while and thought I was intoxicated because of my erratic driving.

For the next 30 minutes, two officers interrogated me and the woman, whose name I never learned, and searched my car, much as you would see on a TV show. In retrospect, it is kind of funny because they could not find anything, not even a biscuit crumb, since my car had been detailed by a church friend that day.

In the end, I am convinced she was, in fact, a prostitute based on what they said, but at least she was honest with them. She told them all she had time to do before they turned on the lights was to ask me for a ride. I am not sure they saw her in the car or they might have given me more time to hang myself. Eventually, they cited her for something, I am not sure what, and sent her on her way. They then cited me for patronizing an area of drugs and prostitution. I was not guilty of trying to buy drugs or engage a prostitute, but I was guilty of plenty more; and that was the moment I felt like life was truly over.

The charge would later be dropped and expunged from my record, and had I not told it a thousand times and on stages and websites, most people would not know about it today. That does not mean I did not sin and it did not happen, and that I was not guilty of being in a place I should not have been and in a condition I should never have let develop. At the moment, it felt like the final nail in a coffin that had been sealing up around me for months. As I look back, it was the wakeup call I needed, and the moment when

I finally realized my life and thinking were both out of control.

I returned home and told my wife, and then met with my staff and leadership to let them know. I offered to resign that day, and they declined while they prayed about it and processed it. About three weeks later, they accepted my resignation, and I asked them to help me figure out where to go from that low point. What I have said to you up until this point, and what we will say in the coming chapters, was hammered out from nothing in this crucible over the next fourteen months.

I was fortunate that the church I had served for nearly nine years was a place of grace and forgiveness and they were willing to do the hard work of helping a broken man find his way back. I am sad to say, that is a very small minority of churches.

Two Extremes

I did not pay much attention before 2008 to how people, and especially churches, treat the people among them who fail in some way. Since then, I have become somewhat of a student of restoration. As I watch both the initial and long-term response of most churches, it makes me so thankful for the church I served at the time. Had either of the two reactions that typically happens when someone fails been applied to me, I certainly would be out of ministry, and I might not be alive. I am grateful for Pastor Mike Dawson, Stan Breeden, Dave Forrester, and our Director of Missions, Dale Ledbetter. All were members of our church, and they became the nucleus of a group of people who refused to give up on me.

Typically, churches, especially the majority that are small and have limited resources, react to a failure in leadership in one of two ways. The first of those is to more or less let it slide. This is the response of the minority of churches, but it happens more often than you might think. The general feeling is one of grace, which is good by the way; but in the name of grace, we choose not to get into the mess at all. Different thoughts drive this position in different churches. They may be thinking that we are a small church and would have a hard time finding another leader. Besides, he has done a good job at everything except this. Other churches may take the position that yes, he messed up, but doesn't the Bible say we should forgive?

The problem with this position is that there is a reason the leader got into the position to fail or break in the first place. Much of what those churches did up to this point is correct. They should have loved and encouraged the offender. They should have exhibited grace and forgiveness. However, letting someone get by with a failure without walking through a process to protect them from future failure is not forgiveness, it is license to do it again.

A friend of mine teaches that everyone has a fault line in his or her life that, left unchecked, will at some point produce an earthquake.[6] I grew up in northwest Tennessee along the New Madrid Fault Line. It lies dormant most of the time, but periodically, as it did in the spring and summer of 2019, it produces an earthquake. Many people understand their spiritual fault line early on and build structures over those fault lines that will stand up and not crumble in an earthquake. If a leader has had some sort of public earthquake in their spiritual journey, it is an indication they need help building a structure into their life that will withstand the earthquake and overcome that fault line.

The other extreme is more common. If they have not been purposely and proactively taught that restoration is the

---

[6] These thoughts are paraphrased and used with permission of FIG Ministries.

work of God, and if the soil has not been sown with grace and forgiveness teaching, those churches just say leave and don't come back. Such churches prefer to never see the offender again. The tragedy of this position is that there is often a root of deeply held bitterness toward that pastor that grows up and bears all kinds of bad fruit. When a person gets bitter toward a former pastor, it becomes increasingly difficult to love another pastor unconditionally. When a church terminates a pastor, even for cause, it gets much easier to fire the next guy. It is a slippery slope, and engaging in the healing process of restoration for a church is a two way street. One mystifying component of the outflow of a root of bitterness is that it affects people who were not even in on the original pain.

"See to it that no one fails to obtain the grace of God; that no 'root of bitterness' springs up and causes trouble, and by it many become defiled" (Hebrews 12:15). Set in the context of an admonishment to strengthen the feeble, and strive for peace and holiness, this teaching underlines the biggest challenges to a church that refuses to engage broken people in restoration. That bitterness toward the former leader will cause trouble. It just does. There may seem to be no connecting line to be drawn from that failure to the current issues plaguing the church, but if there is unforgiveness, there is trouble. The Scripture passage above goes on to say that others will become defiled because of that bitterness. This is why you see churches long after a negative event involving a lay leader or minister still stumbling around, and how even those members who have come since the "event" are caught up in the same cycle.

One of the byproducts of learning this truth was when I began to work with Antioch Church, I realized that while there had not been any major earthquakes to speak of, the church had been dying a slow, painful death for some time. It turned out that in interviews, I discovered a number of pockets of people who were angry at former staff members and pastors, and some at each other, for the way they supported or did not support the former leader. Over a period of about 18 months, we had every living former pastor and staff member back to preach. It gave people a chance to reconnect and work on the forgiveness that was needed.

Restoration Is NOT!

Before we can discuss what restoration is, we have to spend a few minutes talking about what it is not. Restoration is not a promise to put everything back as it was before. It is not a promise to put the offender back in a position of leadership in the church where he or she failed. In fact, it is not a promise that they will ever be back in a position of leadership in a local church. There are too many outside factors for any restoration team or ministry to assure someone they can put them back to work. Certainly, that sometimes happens; but the primary purpose of a restorative process and culture in the church is not to help people get jobs in the church.

For that reason, many professional clergy who have struggled and failed will not participate. It is an indication that they do not understand the purpose of restoration and in fact, may have been just using the process in hopes it would get them "back in the business." The hope of every restorative process is that the failed and broken among us will one day be back in the game; but it might not be on a professional level, and it is rarely back in the same role at the same place where they stumbled. There certainly are times when a person offends a church and they sometime later reconcile and that person again becomes a useful part of the body of Christ; but restoration is not primarily about vocational ministers returning to a paying job.

Richard, who serves alongside me on the staff of Antioch leading our prayer and pastoral care ministry, is a picture of both how difficult and rare it is, but also how beautiful it can be when it happens.[7] Pay careful attention to the times mentioned here. Richard came to be Senior Pastor of Antioch in 1991 and stayed for one year. It was a horrible match and he was not in a good place in his life. Depending on who you ask, he was fired or he resigned in the midst of a separation from his wife and left the area. His wife and children remained at the church and he moved to Texas.

After fourteen years of various staff ministry positions, secular jobs, and life experiences, he came to the realization in 2005 that he had never had a real encounter with Jesus and was beautifully born again into a right relationship with God. In 2011, he moved back in retirement to be near his daughter and grandchildren who had remained in Johnson City for all those years. He asked me for permission to apologize to the church and I affirmed that desire. On Father's Day, 2012, he came back to church for the first time and apologized and shared his testimony of what it meant to be a lost church member and pastor.

The church received him warmly, extended forgiveness, and God was honored as a rift of nearly twenty years began to heal. Afterward, he and his wife, whom he married in 2010, were so well received, they asked if it was possible for them to continue to worship with us. Over a period of time, he began to use some of the skills developed while he was still far from God to help me. He began to fill in for me at chapel services, make some pastoral care visits when I was unavailable, and lead a small group. After a while, it became apparent God had sent him back to us and we embraced him as part of our bivocational staff. One of the most beautiful parts of this is how the oldest of our members who had vilified him for many years are now among his closest friends and most ardent supporters.

---

[7] Story used with permission of Pastor Richard Long.

Take note of how a church that has purposefully begun to cultivate a culture of restoration was able to receive back a pastor who had offended them twenty years earlier. Take note, too, of the fact it was twenty years in the making. Again, it is not impossible to see a pastor or staff member restored to the same body of Christ, but it is not easy and it is not quick.

Barriers

Going into a purposeful season of restoration with a member or minister who has offended or been offended requires a church and a team to recognize there are two sides to every story. Also, it must be recognized that every person sees the event that led to their pain through a different lens, forged by a lifetime of experiences, traditions, and opinions. Understand that just because each party sees it differently does not mean they are lying or deliberately trying to distort the truth. There may be a legitimate disagreement on what actually happened. Trying to figure out who is right and who is wrong is not a function of restoration, and is in fact, a barrier. No matter what happened, sitting in front of you is a broken and hurting person in need of restoration, and you have to decide if they are serious about figuring it out. Trying to declare someone right and wrong is a barrier to restoration and often extends the victim mentality unnecessarily.

Tony Rankin[8] describes that moment as being like the map you encounter at an amusement park. The entire park is sketched out in front of you and there is a big red dot that simply says, "you are here." He goes on to say, it doesn't really matter how you got here. Some came from the Minnie Mouse parking lot and some came from the Donald Duck parking lot, some came in cars and some in trucks; but if you are looking at this sign, you are here and it does not matter how you got here. When it comes to restoration, if you are

---

[8] Used with permission of Tony Rankin, LCT, Nashville, TN.

looking at a broken relationship between a servant and God or a servant and a church, it does not matter how you got here.

There will be much in the process that will allow God to convict of sin, righteousness, and judgment. But YOU are not the judge! If you try to take sides, it will be a barrier to the meaningful conversations that need to come next. One of the toughest early conversations I had with one of the pastors at the church I served was when I told him that I had friends and supporters who would take care of me and he needed to take care of the church. That required both of us to make some difficult decisions, but we remain friends to this day.

The real barriers to restoration can be summed up in three words — theology, tradition, and practicality. There are people spread all along the theological continuum when it comes to deciding if people can ever be restored to usefulness in the church when certain sins are committed. Most of those are sexual and marriage-related, but some are more practical. For instance, we will address in a later chapter the issue of sexual abuse. Our position on a sexual offender is that the church should immediately report the offender to the authorities, and that the person should never be allowed to be in a position of trust again where he or she can re-offend. That does not mean there is no restoration; but it does mean to protect both him and others, we help put some boundaries in his life. Even that is part of restoration. The challenge for the pastor or leader reading this is to have a clear understanding of his own theology when it comes to restoration, and be prepared to teach his people and cultivate the soil, so when the time comes, no one is surprised.

The problem with a clear understanding of our theology of restoration and who can be restored is often our traditions. I am of the Baptist faith and I grew up with some unspoken understandings about what happens when someone has an affair or embezzles money or commits some other crime or sin that becomes public. As I have grown older, I have personally become convinced that many of the barriers to service erected in the church are man-made and based on tradition more than theology. I do think that some things disqualify you from public service in certain roles; but I think we, like our Pharisee friends in the New Testament days, love to add our two cents. Over the years we have begun to practice some religious man-made rules rather than stick to what the Bible says. I am in no way trying to debate your strongly held beliefs, but just saying that when you say someone is beyond either the grace of God or the usefulness of God, be sure you have a Biblical basis for it.

In an earlier chapter, I introduced you to Bill, who rebuilt the transmission in my 2002 Ford Explorer. Think about this. Imagine if after rebuilding or restoring my transmission, Bill had said, "Now, this transmission is as good as new. I have invested hours and hours of painstaking work and sweat equity into it. It is restored, but don't drive it. It is as good as new, but because it failed, it can never be used again, for fear it might fail again." My reaction would have been immediate. What business is it of his what I do with my rebuilt transmission? It is none of your business if I want to take a chance on it and drive it to Alaska! Bill could not tell me what to do with the restored transmission because he is not the owner! Likewise, I cannot tell God what to do with a restored brother or sister because I am not the owner, but just the restorer. God gets to decide what He will do with that restoration project.

Of course, there is the practicality issue in restoration. Pastors and leaders have a responsibility to defend the 99 as much as they do the one. There are times the pain is so new and acute, or the failure is so egregious, that a church simply cannot deal with having the person around. Certainly the pastor has to encourage his church to learn to forgive and move forward, but timing can sometimes dictate that. I suspect bringing Richard back on staff quickly following the separation from Antioch would not have been healthy or even possible.

The church leadership has a responsibility to guard both the reputation and the unity of the church. After all, the world will know we are Christians first by our love for one another and our love for them. Restoration cannot be used to split the church or cause further pain. It is a fine line and one of many places pastors have to consider the greater good. This may seem strange coming from a guy writing about restoration, but my mantra is that the good of the church has to take precedence over the good of any one individual. Even when restoration cannot take place in the church where the offender served, the leaders can often still be involved by networking with other local churches.

Restoration can also be made difficult for a man or woman when the church they have been serving is part of a network of churches in an area where leaders all know each other . Certainly, there is the tension of gossip and raised eyebrows, but most leaders in other churches and in leadership offices are sympathetic to broken people, but they also live in the real world. They are going to have to work with and for the very people who were offended, and to work toward restoration with someone can damage future working relationships. My co-author (Michael) alluded to this in chapter four.

What he did not share was how other local church leaders who knew him reacted. Crickets. No contact, no texts, calls, or emails. But later when Michael served at state children's camps, many of those same leaders approached him to talk and share the stories being circulated. At the time Michael was ousted, stories swirled about what happened and local church leaders stayed away for their own protection. In a neutral setting away from their churches, they felt free to approach Michael and talk about what happened. All were saddened at the stories being perpetuated and how different they were from the facts.

Much of the resistance I get when talking to a church about engaging someone in restoration is around this point. They either think it is impossible, un-Biblical, or impractical to see someone restored to a position of leadership after certain kinds of failure. That is why restoration cannot be about putting someone back to work. In fact, it is also not about putting every previous relationship back the way it was. Every restoration conversation has to begin there. If the only reason someone is willing to submit to this process is so they can get a job, they will not last or the process will be a sham.

So What is Restoration?

We will flesh this out in later chapters as you see the process unfold, but for working purposes, restoration is the sovereign work of God through his church whereby a broken and unusable believer is spiritually repaired and returned to a condition of usefulness to the body of Christ. There is a lot more to it, but we talk about three goals in the restoration process.

The first is to assist the person to understand the faults in their life that led to the public earthquake and build structures to protect them from the next one. To return to Fig Ministries' analogy around Galatians 6:1, we know that faults cause earthquakes. We also know that faults themselves are caused by something that happened in the past. That is true in the earth and true in the lives of believers. Faults under the earth and in our lives can really never be completely repaired. One can, though, build structures over faults that will protect you in case of an earthquake. Earthquakes are going to happen, both physically and spiritually, so we need to be prepared for them. Restoration does not deal with the cause, whether it be childhood trauma, depression, stress, or anything else. Like Tony Rankin said, you are here and it doesn't matter how you got here. Restoration does not try to fix the fault and does not spend a lot of time working on the actual public failure. What restoration does is help a person understand their faults and put structures in place to withstand the coming earthquakes. I was recently told that Japan has more earthquakes and less earthquake fatalities than any nation in the world, because they have learned to build structures that will protect them from the earthquakes.

A second goal of restoration is to build bridges that will help a broken friend reconnect with significant relationships that have been damaged. Certainly, the loss of job and livelihood for a broken minister is at times the most visible damage to his life; but the more significant damage is to the people in his life. The loss of trust and disbelief caused when someone does something radically out of line with past teaching and practice can have devastating effects on the people in their lives. Depending on what actually happened, it can affect spouses, children, old friends, church members, and professional colleagues. All the people the person has depended on to help and support them in times of difficulty are now wounded as well. The promise of restoration is not that all those relationships will be exactly as they were before the event became public, but that the process will build bridges to those people that will allow for healthy and meaningful conversations to occur that will have the potential to create a new normal.

In an earlier chapter, I introduced you to Bill, a lay leader in the church I now serve who slid into drug and alcohol addiction, divorced his wife, and was estranged from his children. He had three former business partners in our church that his problems had nearly bankrupted and they were no longer speaking. He was out of church and living in a self-imposed exile. All the meaningful relationships in his life were shattered, and he was facing life alone. I gathered a team of mature church men who were all old friends of his and we entered a covenant of restoration and walked for eight months with him in that process. Tragically, in his depression, he was prescribed medication that sometimes causes suicidal thoughts. He had been doing fine on another medication and was moving forward, but within a week, he took his own life.

As sad as that story is, in a recent interview with his daughter,[9] she reminded me that the process had re-established communication between her and her dad, her mom had been talking with him, and they had been sharing some meals together. She told of a day before his death when he called her to the house and sincerely apologized for the first time. She spoke forgiveness to him and with some tears, told me that he was her dad for the first time in many years. Despite his death, restoration built bridges to healing in the significant relationships of his life.

Finally, the restoration process itself is valuable to both put a period at the end of a troubling time and serve as a launching point for a new future. Today, ten years after the earthquake in my own life, two things surprise me. One is how few people actually know about it. If I had not written, blogged, and preached about my story, few people would even know. The other thing that surprises me is the people who do know and still bring it up. It does not happen often; but occasionally, I still have a professional colleague or someone in my circle of influence say to me, "Aren't you that preacher that messed up in Nashville a few years ago?" My answer is always the same: "Yes, but let me tell you what I went through and how it has changed my life."

Certainly, haters are gonna hate, but the process itself allows people to see that you recognize you needed help and you submitted to a process that offered you that help. When you tell people that it was not just a two-hour counseling

---

[9] Interview with Elizabeth Cox in April, 2019.

session, but a 12-18 month process that helped you reconnect with God and the people you hurt, they have to at least admit you took it seriously.

Before You Move On

For me, the process helped me find and define a fault line of codependency and people pleasing in my life that I did not know was there. There is a reason it is there but the reason does not matter. What does matter is that I had this fault and got overtaken in this fault by a fast-growing church that grew beyond the point where I could keep everyone happy. I let that consume me and eventually flamed out. AGAIN, I make no excuses. I sinned! The process, though, helped me understand and build some structures over that fault line.

I have returned to the pastorate and God has used me. There are still people that tell me from time to time that I should not be in this position. That is their theology and tradition and I don't think it is personal, although at times it stings. I have quit reading people's posts about me and listening to gossip about me or anyone else, because I have this understanding of what restoration is and what it is not.

For Further Thought:

1. Take some time to consider your own theology of restoration. What do you believe about the responsibility for you and your church, the limits of restoration, and what are the questions you have about those things?

2. Are there traditions from your own life and faith background that make you skeptical of the process of restoration? Spend some time considering which of them are Biblical and which are traditional.

3. Who do you know in your church and under your influence that currently are separated from the significant relationships of their past due to their own failures?

Chapter 7

Restoration is Messy!

Restoration is messy work! That may be the "Captain Obvious" quote of this entire book. There is a reason most churches do not proactively work toward helping wounded, broken, and self-destroyed pastors and leaders get back on their feet. We have discussed some of them already.

It is distasteful. Many of those leaders have committed sins that honestly, in our opinion, are worse than the ways in which we sin. We don't say that out loud, but we feel it.

It is time consuming, and every pastor and church leader is already overwhelmed with the weekly cycle of ministry and the "other duties as assigned" that consume our days.

Yet the biggest obstacle to restorative ministry in a local church is that it is just messy. There are too many different agendas and too many opposing needs among the networks of those who have flamed out in some way. Maybe my story can help us understand the ways it gets messy.

When Bad Becomes Worse

In an earlier chapter, I told you the story of my flameout years ago. With ten years of recovery, and now, nine years of personal restoration and restorative ministry under my belt, I have the benefit of 20/20 hindsight. This part of the story is more painful than what I have already written, because at any moment, in any stage of the journey, I could have done one thing differently; and the end result could and probably would have been dramatically different. Like you, I believe in the sovereignty of God, and that all things do in fact work together for good to those who love God. But looking back, none of the mistakes I made and sins I committed during those last 60 days were from God. I suspect we too quickly say, "God must have wanted that to happen since it has opened this door to current ministry."

I do believe with all my heart that God can take my mess and turn it into a message. But make no mistake about it — in the final days of this depression, I was walking in my own power, not in the Spirit. With the benefit of 10 years of looking back, I am convinced that much of the depression was caused by my distance *from* God, far more than my depression caused me to distance *myself* from God.

Again, let me disclaim that by saying if you need help, see a doctor. Depression is real, but it can be a vicious cycle. You start sliding into a depression and then get distant from God, and begin to lose touch with the disciplines of your faith. Before you know it, the depression is worse. Now, you find yourself fighting the most difficult battle of your life without the intimate involvement and direction of your loving Father.

The core issue of my failure in that season, though I could not put it into words until many years later, was my pride. I have never battled the pride that makes me feel like I am better than anyone else, but my pride is rooted in a desire to keep my shortcomings secret so no one will know how I really am.

At my most successful moments in ministry, I always had this nagging sense that I was not good enough and would never measure up to other people. I believed that if they really knew how hard I had to work to appear successful, they would not want to follow me. Psychotherapists would probably look at my upbringing and give you a list of reasons for that, but the bottom line is that it is one area where I went 25 years of my adult life and ministry without letting God deal with it. As with all secrets, it eventually came out in a very public way.

That was the pride that let me continue to meet with an accountability partner, but would not let me be transparent with him. That pride was the reason I rejected my wife's plea to see a doctor. That pride kept me from meeting with a local counselor to whom I had referred people in great numbers because of his giftedness. That pride caused me to continue trying to be a "superman" pastor out of codependency, causing me to need to please everyone.

Toward the end, I found myself looking for an escape, any escape. I talked to people on my staff and in my circle, but was never truly honest with them about the depth of the despair I felt. On one occasion, I was so far gone, and though I would not have thought so then, was even suicidal, I spoke to my executive pastor to try to communicate how desperately I needed help. Even then, I could not let him know how badly I was struggling, so I spoke in such guarded terms that he had no way or impetus to help me. For a long time, I was angry with him because I thought I had asked him for help, but I put him in a no-win situation. I did not give him enough information to make the right decision. I have since cleared the air with him and we remain friends, but that was one of the places where I could have done something to avoid the earthquake that was to come.

Because of that, my life was a mess. I was a picture of the proverbial swan, floating along peacefully as far as anyone knew; but underneath, paddling as hard as I could, and losing momentum all the time. Then "it" happened — that fateful night in July of 2008 that brought my world to a halt. Being accused of something I did not do that was so big and ugly, that I had no choice but to be honest about other things that were true of my life. This seems to be the only way God could get my attention. I believe now that night was both the discipline of God and the rescue of God. However, my life was about to get messy.

Think with me for a moment about the mess that surrounded my life and the reason that kind of mess makes restoration difficult for a pastor or church.

A Life in Shambles

It is messy for both the person in need of restoration and the people working toward restoration, if that is indeed happening. Consider my life as an example. When I first met with my restoration team, I had resigned my church job, had no resources and no marketable skills other than pastoring, had disappointed church people who loved me, had placed my family in a state of flux, and was even more depressed than before. From the outside, you would have been hard pressed to find any reason for me, of all people, to be depressed prior to the meltdown, because I had covered it well. However, after I lost my job, for the first time, I had a real reason for depression.

I remember sitting down at my desk on a Monday morning after I stepped away from the pulpit and before they accepted my resignation, and realizing for the first time in my adult life I had nowhere to go, no one depending on me, and nothing to prepare. At the same time, I did not know who among my professional friends and colleagues would still be willing to be around. For a codependent person whose pride was fed by being needed and capable and having people around all the time, this was a watershed moment. I had NOTHING to do. I could not recover and could not prove myself to anyone. I was alone, or at least felt alone. I was a mess because my life was in shambles. I remember one day walking through the house in my pajamas and working on a jigsaw puzzle at 1 pm, thinking to myself, "this is like One Flew Over the Cuckoo's Nest."

When a pastor or church takes on a restoration project, they take up all the mess that goes with that person's life. I did not need my team to fix all those things, but they had to be involved in all of them. I was convinced my only hope was to get a church job somewhere if anyone would have me, and the restoration team had to tell me I could not do that. I had issues to resolve and processes to put in place before I would be able to return to vocational ministry, if ever. That is just one example, but they had to get involved in the mire of my failure to both understand it and help me figure a way out of it.

A Time Consuming Mess

My worship pastor often says to me that a dilemma we face at the church is a "crockpot, not a microwave" issue. I doubt that line is original to him, but I hear it a lot. This is true of restorative ministry as well. Gordon MacDonald, in his book, *Building Below the Waterline*,[10] talks much about the difference in our public and private ministry. While the public ministry may have just suffered a cataclysmic event that brought about the need for restoration, it is extremely rare that a public failure is not a result of a long period of things happening below the waterline. There is really never an easy fix in restoration, and there is usually a lot of tension around it.

Typically, you have a pastor/staff member who despite having suffered a failure or having been mistreated or becoming collateral damage to someone else's sin, still feels a call and even a compulsion to be engaged in vocational ministry. While there may be some rare instance out there somewhere of someone who has been publicly embarrassed by failure who needs to continue in their ministry role during the time of the restoration process, I have yet to see one. Can you see the tension developing?

---

[10] Gordon MacDonald, *Building Below the Waterline* (Hendrickson Publishing, July 8, 2011).

For me, I was honestly stunned when my team required that I engage in no ministry role other than service without their permission. Having spoken in front of hundreds of groups, thousands of times, and having spent my life honing that skill, I felt muzzled. Yet, they were clear headed enough to realize that I would not have the time or desire to do the hard work without stepping away from that enabling limelight.

In the context of this, it most often involves the ability of the person being restored to make a living. He or she feels the tension of needing to get back to a living wage, and the easiest way to get there is to find a ministry job. For the restoration team who loves that person enough to invest this time in them, it means living with the tension of doing the right thing rather than the expedient thing.

On a more practical note, it is a time consuming mess to a team of men or women who are already overworked and stretched too thin. For my team, it meant taking another 3-5 hours a month to pray, meet with me, review my progress, check up on me, and put up with me calling them, because while they were busy, I was not. I am convinced that much restoration does not happen in the local church simply because of the amount of time it requires. A team has to be developed, a process has to be put in place, meetings have to be scheduled, reviews have to be done, pastoral care has to be offered, and the list goes on. Our prayer in writing this book is to give you a head start and save you some of that time.

The Stakeholder's Mess

In chapter two, I introduced you to Bill, an old friend, who was so busy working for God that he lost the intimacy with God he once enjoyed, and it led to a spiral that cost him ministry, relationships, his business, and his family. Years later, when I and a team from my church began to walk with him in the process of restoration, I discovered very personally how difficult it can get for the stakeholders in a person's life. This difficulty can make it even more messy for the pastor or church who would come alongside that person and try to offer a hand up out of the mess they find themselves in. Consider some of those stakeholders and how the tension might make restoration difficult.

Personal Stakeholders

Family dynamics are different in each situation. I was very fortunate because my wife and my two college-age children (at that time) were understanding and did not reject nor abandon me. However, that does not mean they were not affected by it. One of the most difficult moments and memories of this season was saying goodbye to my son as he left on a mission trip in Romania, knowing that he would be halfway around the world when I announced my resignation. He knew something was wrong but did not know the seriousness of it. Yet, like every family that suffers trauma or loss, my wife and children suffered because of my need for restoration.

Not all those who need us to help them are so fortunate. Often that is because the family has been in on the secret for a long time and have been forced to keep the secret. When the person in need of restorative ministry is one who has been wronged by the church, the family wants nothing to do with the church, and fears that restoration will lead them back into that fishbowl existence as a pastor's family. Michael's family still feels the effect of how he was treated all these years later, making it difficult to even attend church, much less return to active service.

The ripple of wounded relationships typically goes beyond the immediate family. It affects in-laws, long-standing family friendships, and relationships within the church where they served. Coupled with the immediate family dynamics, these broken relationships make restoration a messy process. It is one of the reasons we stress in restoration that the process is not about putting things back the way they were, either professionally or personally; it is about building bridges between the broken and their loved ones that will allow newer, healthier relationships to result.

For the pastor or church leader attempting to lead the broken through a restorative process, he or she can get caught up between agendas. It is good to remember here, as in sharing the gospel, that your job is to lead the process but let the Holy Spirit do the work. I have met children and wives who say they will never forgive their husband or father or the church that mistreated them. While never is a long time, some of them have held onto their position doggedly. The messiness of a broken man or woman who is genuinely repentant and wanting to make amends and their former relationships that will not heal is perhaps the greatest challenge to this journey. We just have to learn to live with that mess.

For my old friend, Bill, I have witnessed up close and personal the pain and the mess his failure caused. With their permission, I am telling you their story. I see his ex-wife every week as she worships and volunteers in the church office. She never wanted to be anything but Bill's wife, but he let her down. She never wanted to divorce him, but how many times can you ignore or forgive such egregious sins? When I began to put together his team, some of the questions asked were could he come back to our church and was she willing for our church to help him toward restoration? I saw the hurt in her life when she said she was not ready to see him at her church every week. The church had been her only anchor during the past decade, and to have him there reminding her of all she lost was just too much.

As the process unfolded over the next eight months, she softened toward him and they began to have dinner together, and she compassionately helped him with some things that, in his failing health, he could not do on his own. Who knows what would have happened except for his untimely death? But there was no mistaking the messiness of the church and me being involved in this process. I was careful of her and her feelings while trying to coach and pastor him. Even today, years after his death, I see the pain caused by that season. She struggles in so many ways because of the decisions he made.

His daughter, Elizabeth, sat down with me for an interview during the writing of this book. I have known her since she was a little girl. She has grown into a wonderful and Godly young wife, and by the time this is published she will be a mother. Yet years past his failure, she spoke with tears about how her faith in God and the church were rattled by his double life. She told of catching him in his sin and feeling unable to talk to anyone about it. Like her mother, she clings to a moment of forgiveness and healing between them just before his death, but still feels deeply the pain and the ramifications of his failure. I married her and her husband a short time after his death, and remember her tears that day. We were both thinking that Dad should have been here; and if he had made different choices along the way, he probably would have been. As her pastor, I had to live with the tension of her deep pain and her dad's restoration process.

In dealing with many families with similar dynamics, I have discovered the key is honesty and communication. Too often, when people are being restored, the family stakeholders are left to feel that they are being shuttled aside and their feelings don't matter. For the pastor who is walking through a restoration process with either a wounded or failed pastor or lay leader, a key is acknowledging the mess of the surrounding familial relationships and working very hard to not make demands or place undue expectations on anyone. I have had more than one family member say that everyone is so excited to see change in the offender, it feels like they are being told their pain is not valid and they just need to get over it.

Professional Stakeholders

In addition to family stakeholders, there are professional stakeholders. My meltdown not only hurt my family, but there are hundreds of former church members and leaders who were left to ask why. I did not hear this personally, but a friend told of a pastor's wife who was in his shop after my failure became public. She asked the question, "If this can happen to him, is anyone exempt or safe? How do I know my husband won't be next?" Of course, we know the answer is that any of us can fail or be wounded at any time, but consider the reality that the wife of a professional colleague felt the ripple effect of my decisions.

Pastors and denominational leaders often walk a tightrope of restoration and concern for the wounded. Already, Michael has written for you some of the ways he felt isolated even though he really did nothing wrong. Mission leaders for denominations are affected when a friend or colleague is hurt by one of the leader's churches or hurts one of their churches. The leader may know some things that the restoration team or church does not yet know, or may have heard a very different version of the story from the "other side." Regardless, those leaders within the circle of the person needing restoration find themselves at least in an uncomfortable position, if not worse. Thus, the church or pastor that wants to restore a broken brother may find an unexpected mess in denominational or collegial relationships. It is part of the cost that must be counted.

Even lay leaders who fail leave a mess behind them professionally. When my friend, Bill, was in a freefall, he led some men in our church to go into business with him. Due to his drug abuse and other hidden vices, he led them into bankruptcy. All of those men are still working long past the age of retirement due to his decisions. One of those men attends our church. Because he and his wife are of great faith, they were willing to see restoration; but it is clear they have a mess caused by Bill that they are left to clean up into their 70s. Caring for them as we began to care for Bill was a necessary step in the process.

On a personal note, I had assembled a capable and talented staff, and for the most part, we worked very well together. I let them down. It was particularly painful for some of them to know I was still around, but could not lead them, and truly could not spend much time with them, so they could get used to a new leader. Years later, most of those relationships have been restored, but it was not without causing them significant pain.

Church Members

I won't go into detail here, but every church leader, either lay or professional, that has an event that leads to removal from their position leaves behind church members at all levels of maturity who are affected by it. Young believers often quit going to that church, and sometimes any church, because they are so disappointed in the leader or the people who pushed them away. Senior saints are often torn between their love for the leader and their disappointment in what he did. Others have their preconceived notions of church being harsh and harmful validated, even though most churches are far from that.

For me, I think of the young men who were disappointed in me. Because of my process, I was not allowed to keep in touch with them in any meaningful way. I still think looking back that was the best way to handle it, but I know it affected their spiritual journey.

Like Ripples on a Pond

In my experience, it has been impossible to truly count the cost of restoration in advance, especially in the area of how much mess you will encounter. As a boy, like most boys, I enjoyed throwing rocks into our farm ponds. Long after the rock hits the water, those waves are still lapping up against the shore somewhere. If you got hit by the rock, you would be more affected than if you just got hit by the wave, but either way you are affected. Think about the messes you may encounter in restoration like those waves and ripples. The closer you are to the center of the event, the more it will affect you; but even those further out suffer some effects from the event.

You just have to acknowledge that you are going to find a mess, and you will probably step in that mess somewhere along the way, despite your best intentions. For us and our teams, we talk about that a great deal, and just learn to say "Well, that was a mess, wasn't it?" You can't predict the mess perfectly and you can't fix every mess you encounter. However, you can know it is going to be messy and go in with your eyes open.

Flying Under the Radar

Restorative ministry is messy and for that reason, much of it takes place hidden from the eyes of almost everyone. In fact, many members of the church I serve have been surprised I was writing a book on restorative ministry because it is so low-key. I have mentioned several stakeholders in this chapter, and you have to consider those needs, but not everyone has to be in on every decision. Restoration really is a "need-to-know" basis kind of ministry. For instance, if Bill's ex-wife had not been a friend and church member, I would not have consulted her. I always include my deacons and staff and any church members affected by the process, but most people just don't need to know. When people are wounded, they may not know the right thing to do, and may hinder the valuable work of healing and restoration.

Before You Move On

By any worldly standard, restoration work is messy and we fail more often than not. People think they want to go through the process, but when they find out the level of commitment necessary, they back out. Others just quit midstream because it is too hard. For others, they have a different agenda and are not ready to get real with God, self, and the team. Regardless, it is not a high percentage game. You just have to satisfy yourself knowing that you are doing what God led you to do, and being thankful for that one or two or however many who make it through the process.

For Further Thought:

1. Can you think of a time when you personally threw a lifeline to someone who had been injured by a church or who had injured the church and found yourself enduring some unintended consequences? What would you do differently if given that opportunity again? Have you been more cautious about restoration ministry as a result?

2. Have you personally been affected by a crisis in another church leader's life? In retrospect, were you more grace-filled or more judgmental?

3. Who are some people in your sphere of influence today that are messy but in need of your help? Are there people in your congregation who have been wounded deeply that you

might encourage, even as the one who offended them is being restored?

Chapter 8

The Process is Personal

The reason restoration happens so infrequently is that an individual may lean that way, but often does not operate in a culture that is open to help those who have flamed out or burned out. The next section of this book is about how to develop a culture of restoration. Before we move on, let's talk about the intensely personal nature of restorative ministry.

We talk much in today's church world about the chronically de-churched. Although that is a descriptor of a group of people in our communities, it in no way communicates all the different things that have happened or problems that have occurred to cause people to become de-churched. I meet almost as many de-churched people in my community as I do those that don't believe in God or just don't want to go to church. They are de-churched because a pastor disappointed them, a spouse left them, a parent abandoned them, a church wounded them, or any number of other reasons. All of them have somehow equated that with God and chosen to blame the church. Each of those de-churched individuals need a different approach if they are to be won back to the church and to Christ.

Just as you can't treat all de-churched people in your community the same, you cannot treat all those in need of restoration the same. We devoted a whole chapter earlier to who needs restoration. As you may have noticed throughout this book, even these authors struggle with terminology to define them. Some are wounded and some have failed; some have burned out and some have flamed out; some have left God and family and home and others have just faded off into the sunset. Some have sexual sin and others suffer from emotional illness; some were fired for incompetence and some were fired for no reason at all; while some have healthy support systems, some are all alone.

Even though the ultimate purpose of this book is to put in your hands a process-driven model of restoration, it is important to note that not every person benefits from the same process. To that end, we have provided you a framework from which you can adapt an individually specific process for each of those people as the need arises.

Everyone does not need everything, but some need it all. Others will need parts of the restoration process from you while getting their counseling needs or accountability support in another place. Try to avoid the one-size-fits-all mentality and be open to addressing the needs specific to that situation.

One Common Need

There is, however, one need that every person who needs restoration has in common. Each one needs a safe place to work on what the new normal is going to look like. When your failure is public, even if it is not caused by you, it is normal to struggle to walk into stores where you have always shopped and go to places you've always frequented, even the church. You constantly live with a niggling idea in the back of your mind that if I go in there, I am going to encounter someone that is going to talk about "that" event that led you to where you are now. If a person is unfairly treated, they begin to ask, "Whose side are they on?" If the person has had a moral or personal failure of some kind, they wonder what that person is thinking and if they even will speak to them. It becomes easier to just move away if possible, or if not, just isolate.

This is where a church and a pastor can meet a need, even if they never engage in an active ministry of restoration. A church and a pastor that are predisposed toward loving

those who have disappointed others is more than halfway to
becoming a place of restoration. When a broken and
wounded brother or sister feels isolated and abandoned or
embarrassed, having a pastor who not only says it is okay for
you to hang out with him and his church, but that he really
wants you to do so, is a lifeline in a stormy sea.

When my family and I (Michael) left West Tennessee to
return home and move in with family, none of us wanted to
talk about church, much less attend one. And my family
graciously let us lay in bed on Sundays with no pressure or
judgment while they rose early and went to their church. Pete
(my co-author) is a pastor who reached out to us early on to
provide tangible assistance when we needed a vehicle after
ours was repossessed. No judgment or pressure, or sense of
obligation to attend his church; simply "Here's a guy I know
who can help you get into a vehicle right away." Pete had
somehow heard of our situation and spoke to a member of
his church who could help, arranging for him to assist us.

Pete also agreed that we may feel comfortable in a
church, when we were ready, different from Antioch, and
referred us to a nondenominational church planting network
in the area which we eventually joined. We are still not regular
attenders, and I have been a guest at Antioch where Pete
serves as pastor. Both churches offered the opportunity to sit
and receive ministry with no pressure and no obligation. The
wounds in my heart and in my family are far from healed; but
Pete and the pastor of the other local church have been
steady in their love and care for us with no strings attached.

When I (Pete) left my church, we were committed to
attending church somewhere. At that time, I had been
pastoring the largest church in my county and could not go to
any church where I would not know someone. I am sure
there were pastors and laypersons who would have loved me,
not judged me, and welcomed me with open arms. Yet, very

few actually said this to me. When you are as low as I was emotionally, your mind starts to play tricks on you, and you wonder if those colleagues really even cared for you, or if they just hung around with you so you could help them with something. I do not for a minute believe this was true in retrospect, but at that time, my thinking was far from clear.

I even had some conversation with my restoration team regarding attending the church where I was serving prior to the crash, and of course, they said no. I did not understand it at the time, but that was wise. However, it also reinforced in me the dire feeling that no one would ever care about me, now that I could not serve them.

In the first weeks of this journey, we visited with several churches just north of us, choosing large churches and arriving late, sitting on the back row, and deliberately not identifying ourselves. In short, we were every pastor's nightmare — visitors that refused to be known. Then one Saturday, a well-known pastor in the area called me on the phone.

To this day, I can tell you almost word-for-word what he said: "Pete, I just heard you resigned. I don't know what happened, and I don't care what happened. You and Lori are going to need a safe place for a while, so why don't you come worship with us? If you want a place to serve or a place to be anonymous, just let me know. If you need an office to work out of while you figure out your next steps, you can have one here. Whatever we can do to help, we want to help."[11]

The next morning, my wife and I walked into that huge church with the wide hallways, multiple venues, and milling crowd. We were 100 feet down the hallway when the pastor saw us. He walked toward us and hugged us and told us how

---

[11] Pastor Rick White, The People's Church, Franklin, TN.

glad he was to see us. As much as I needed discipline, reproof, and instruction, I needed a safe place to worship and repent without the judging eyes of those who disapproved of me and only knew what they heard.

In the months that followed, while not being allowed or even wanting to preach or teach or lead any kind of study, we joined a home group and met with a prayer team that prayed during one of the services each week. When your whole sense of identity and belonging are caught up in the church you serve, and that has been yanked out from under you, having a place where they were expecting to see you and glad you were there made all the difference in the world. That church had no official assignment in my restorative process, but having a place to call home and feel safe made it possible to endure the hard work of restoration.

It All Starts With You

Long before you face the need to restore a broken brother or sister in your fellowship or your circle of influence, you can work on being a person who does not judge the fallen and is willing to be seen as their friend, even if there is a personal cost. As we get into this discussion further in the next section, you will hear about how to develop that culture of restoration. But let me point out here that it is caught more than taught, and it has to flow from the top down.

We have a unique restoration story on our church staff. A few years ago, a family that had been involved in the situation 30 years ago with this pastor attended a homecoming service. When they found out he was back on staff, they were curious. I did not want to get into it too deeply, but just said to them, in the presence of one of my 75-year-old deacons, that Antioch is a place of healing and restoration. That older deacon, who is very supportive of the ministry, said quickly, "That is more about Pete than it is

Antioch." To this day, I am not sure if he was just hedging his bets or trying to compliment me; but he was right about one thing — the pastor has a great deal to do with how a church views restoration.

I don't tell you that to brag on me, but to point out that your church family will pick up their verbal cues from you. If you believe that failed church leaders are beyond the grace of God and can never be used anywhere in the church again, your church will pick up on your nonverbal clues and have the same attitude. Even if you are willing to accept those that come your way, but never reach out to them, your church will assume they are beyond the reach of God's grace and not be a place that is accepting when and if one of them accidentally finds your church.

If restoration rather than abandonment is going to be the direction of your church, you will have to lead by example. Be that guy that goes out of his way to call a brother 30 miles away and say, "I don't know what happened, and I don't care what happened; I love you, and you are welcome here."

Re-defining the Win

As we have said, the needs and the process are vastly different even though the primary need for a safe place to heal and recover is a universal need. The pathways to needing restorative ministry are as varied as the pathways out of it. This is just one more way that restoring broken people is incredibly hard. If the person seeking restoration has only one desire, for everything to be put back the way it was, he or she is going to be greatly disappointed. Likewise, if a pastor or church sees the only win as being where the marriage is reunited or the minister is restored to vocational ministry, and everyone lives happily ever after, they are destined to be frustrated and grow disillusioned with restoration. The truth is, I have seen very few people whose life went back to what it was before the event.

I have a great story of God's grace, but much of what my life was like prior to 2008 is long gone. Some of the things that were not restored cause me much pain. Some of the things that I once thought were critical to my success I am now glad were not restored. Sadly, a number of friendships have not been restored at all, and the ones that have been restored are not the same. They could not be the same, as they were rooted in my role as their pastor and overseer, and I am no longer in that role.

Michael is doing incredibly well in his freelance writing career and in his journey with God, but his relationship with the church in general and that church in particular has never been the same and likely may never be the same. It has affected his family deeply, through no fault of his or theirs, and the spiritual trajectory of their family has been affected.

I am simply saying that a church and a pastor that wants to tackle the wonderfully rewarding work of restorative ministry must also be aware that it can be incredibly frustrating. While I am not a researcher and I have a very narrow research sample, my experience is that only about one out of three actually return to vocational ministry if that is what they did before. Overall, about half of the people who enter into a restoration covenant with us finish the process and would describe themselves as meaningfully reintegrated into the church. We define that as being in a place where they are growing spiritually, serving regularly, using their spiritual gifts to minister to others in some way, and feeling fulfilled as a believer.

I have a young deacon in my church who is a high school baseball and softball coach and loves baseball. I tease him mercilessly about the obscure and arcane statistics baseball announcers rely on to fill interminably long gaps between actual action. I tell him that baseball is 9 ½ minutes of action packed into 3 ½ hours, so they have to have something to talk about. So why not talk about meaningless trivia? It makes his blood pressure go up just a little.

I have always been amazed that they give multimillion dollar contracts to hitters who only get on base ⅓ of the time. That means they fail ⅔ of the time. Yet, here I am telling you that in restorative ministry, you are an all-star if you have that kind of winning percentage. Don't get discouraged by the numbers.

From the beginning of each restorative ministry covenant process, consider the outcome that is realistic and possible. Celebrate the little wins. Be willing to strike out a lot. Be satisfied with a long single or advancing the other runners from time to time. No matter how badly you want the home run every time, remember the person in need of restoration is God's property, and He alone gets to decide how to use him or her. Your purpose is to be an instrument in God's hands to do the work that God wants to do.

Church Attendance/Involvement May Be Enough

The most common frustration with those either in the restorative process or having completed it is the lack of deep roots in the local church. Don't be surprised by that. Most of us, including me, have never had to look for a church before. When we were at the church, we did not have to look for the right place to serve. Most of us went from church to church based on our calling and employment opportunities. We did not need to find a place to serve, since we were called to a special place of service at that church.

Some are so wounded they can never trust the church enough to really dig in. Realistically, many of those who never plug in and serve simply don't know how to do that. For that reason, a restorative process needs to include some assistance in choosing a church that the team knows will give appropriate oversight, and then including accountability for that in the process. I did not know until some time later that a member of my restoration team reached out to that pastor about calling me. It was in his nature anyway, so he was not prompted about what to say. But he had not heard and would not have called without a prompt from my restoration team.

Restorative churches need to be a place where men and women who don't know how to choose a church or serve in a volunteer position, because they've never done so, can find their way. It will include such things as working with people in your church to do what that pastor did. If you see some giftedness in them that can be used while they are going through the process without harming the process, talk to those leading that ministry in your church and have them reach out. Afterward, follow up with the team to see if the candidate responded appropriately.

Obedience Is Its Own Reward

So few finish the process, and fewer still are actually restored to vocational or significant service, it is easy to get frustrated and throw in the towel. Yet, there is that pesky Galatians 6:1 telling us to restore those who have been ambushed by sin. When we engage in restoration, there are so many ways it can go south that we have to be satisfied to just know we are doing the Lord's work, and rejoice in those few processes that turn out well.

You also have to be in it with a Kingdom mindset. I did not think this through when we began to pray and shape Antioch into a place of restoration, but most people who successfully complete a covenant restoration process will not stay in your church, if they ever come there at all. Some will leave because they get back on their feet and God puts them back in a ministry role somewhere. Some will leave because they felt you were too hard on them in the process.

Truthfully, some will leave because they don't want or don't know how to submit to spiritual authority, having always been the spiritual authority. That may give you a hint as to why they need you in the first place. Others will leave for the same reason that many who you pastor through a marriage crisis leave. You just know too much about them and it is hard to face you every week; even though most of us have learned long ago that people are not defined by their problems. We don't even think about that issue, but they are worried that we think negatively toward them. If you do not practice restoration as an offering to the Lord, it is a very thankless ministry.

Before You Move On

Go into it with your eyes open, be flexible, and celebrate whatever God does. When you do that, there is no greater celebration among God's children than to be able to help one and then celebrate like the father of the prodigal son that "he was lost, and is found."

For Further Thought:

1. When have you had to adapt processes in your church and professional life to accomplish the greater good? Was it difficult for you to do? What was the result?

2. Do you have a good reading of the temperature about restoration in your own life and church? Write down some examples of times you have befriended believers who have had a public fall of some kind. Do you tend to do that more

for those that are offended than for the offender? Do you have examples of your church reaching out to a fallen brother or sister?

3. Do you know how to look for a church and/or find a place to serve in a local church? Do you know a pastor who has been between church assignments and struggled to find a place to land or even when they did, struggled to fit in? What have you done to help them?

Chapter 9

Restoring the Sexually Broken vs. the Sexual Predator

In this section of the book, we have aimed at helping you see the need, and possibility of healing, for not only the spiritually wounded in the church, but also those who have wounded others and now desire to be restored. Remember the prodigal son had an "aha" moment and came to his senses in the pig pen. We need to accept that restoration is possible for anyone, and that no one is beyond the grace of God.

Every broken follower of Christ is a candidate for restoration when their life runs aground. Even as I write these words, I can hear the chorus of "amens" coming from readers. Yet, within the church, sexual sin is the one sticking point for many. We acknowledge that God may forgive them, but many of our denominational and faith backgrounds have forged in us an unspoken understanding that one who is in a church leadership position and commits a sexual sin can never be used to serve in any leadership position again.

I acknowledge that some of what you are about to read is controversial, so I ask that you receive it with two ideas in mind. First, do not read any more into it than is in black and white print. I often tell my church when I cover a difficult subject, "Please hear what I am saying and not what I am not saying. I don't mind you getting mad over what I say; but don't get mad at what I did not say." Second, remember that I have told you from the beginning, restoration is not necessarily nor always restoration to a ministry position. And it certainly is almost never restoration to the ministry position and location they held when the sin was committed or the schism occurred. With that in mind, and with some fear and trepidation on my part, let's tackle this difficult subject.

A Sticking Point

This is another one of those places where the wheels can run off and you may be tempted to throw away this book because you disagree. Try not to do that. You have worked too hard to get here, so hang on.

Do you remember the story about having my transmission rebuilt in my old Explorer? The mechanic who fixed it had no right to tell me how to use it. I approach this subject in the same way. If a man has suffered a divorce or family rift of some kind, and comes to me in genuine repentance and in need of restoring, I do all I can to help him get back on his feet. I also hold the results very loosely, letting God decide whether he restores them to vocational ministry or not.

For instance, I have a friend in our community, I'll call him Jerry,[12] who is not a member of my church but has a unique story. He married young but then left his wife, I'll call her Malinda, after a few years to sow some wild oats. Both he and his wife remarried quickly and divorced quickly. Sometime later, he and she came to their senses, both found their way to God, and they ultimately remarried. He now lives in my community, but the events above happened when they lived hundreds of miles away. In the 40+ years they have lived in the Tri-Cities, he has come to be viewed as a Godly statesman and faithful husband. Yet, there are still people back in his home church that know him as the guy who left his wife and squandered his youth. Everyone is entitled to their own opinion, but here is mine. If I were his current pastor, I would probably use him in a leadership role, since he is clearly a one-woman man, and has been for many years, possesses a stellar reputation, and is already doing the work of a servant. However, in the little church back home, his

---

[12] Used with permission. Names have been changed.

reputation may never be spotless again; so in that location, I might not. In other words, let's do the work of restorative ministry and let God do with people what He will.

On a more personal note, I was given the opportunity to be a campus pastor in the community where I lived and pastored when I blew out in 2009. The lead pastor of the mother ship was a part of my restoration process and knew all the details. He was willing to take a chance on me and believed I was the best fit for the role since I knew the area. However, even though I was not guilty of sexual sin, I had been accused of patronizing a known area of drugs and prostitution. Even though I was investigated, and the charges were dropped and my record expunged, it does not matter what I did or did not do in the minds of many. Accusation is tantamount to guilt. At the very least, I am clearly not a man of good reputation and above reproach in that community. I chose not to pursue the conversation because it is hard enough to win people to Christ when they don't have a little doubt in the back of their minds about your character.

On the other hand, a church that I had served as a staff member several years earlier called me to be their pastor 18 months later. Even though they were in the same state, the first thing I had to do was tell them the whole sordid story. I also directed them to call the men who served on my restoration team and check me out with the deacons and leadership of the church I left. For the first time ever, I was disappointed in the Baptist grapevine. They had known me for 25 years and to this day, I enjoy a residual good reputation in the community that I probably don't deserve.

I felt qualified to be their pastor even though I did not feel qualified to serve the new campus church. This is a simple illustration of the fallacy of the hardline positions we take. The reason we do it is that it is often easier to just make a one-time decision about everyone that is accused of a sexual sin, or those who divorce and remarry, than it is to get in the mess with them and help them find healing and purpose with God. As a pastor and leadership team, we all have the right and responsibility to decide for ourselves what we will do, but we cannot limit God in what He can and might do with someone you or I deem unqualified.

The Elephant in the Room

In today's climate of the #metoo movement, even the church has been caught up in the exposure of decades of predatory ministers and pastors that remained hidden and covered up. Instead of dealing with those predators, the church often just fired them and encouraged those predators to move on down the road, which freed them to reoffend, often multiple times. Some denominations and faiths have better track records than others on this matter, but I think we can all agree that we are better off having ripped the cover off that hidden cesspool so we could deal with it and repent of it. I am not going to write much more about that topic, but I do want to acknowledge that it makes restoration of anyone caught in any kind of sexual sin more difficult.

Here is my opinion. I believe it is a Biblical position and you are free to disagree with me. That does not negate the rest of the book and the need for restoration ministry in your life and church. You decide who you think is a candidate for restoration and do that work.

My opinion is that the sexually broken, those who have had an affair, been caught up in pornography, fallen into same sex relationships and the like, can be restored to usefulness in the Kingdom of God. That does not mean they will return to church leadership where they were, or certainly not quickly. Their leadership role may be in another area of ministry altogether, but I do not believe sexual sin forever disqualifies a man or woman from all future service to the church. I believe they have to repent, put safeguards in place, and prove themselves over a long period of time, but there are also places God can use their spiritual gifts throughout the process. One of the reasons so many pastors never get rooted in a church after being overtaken in a sin, is that they are not allowed to do anything. Most of us in ministry know that a person who just sits in the worship event each week and has no assignment or connection is not going to be around long.

I also believe it is possible for the sexual predator who comes to his senses, confesses his brokenness and sinfulness, gets psychological help, and goes through a long and specialized process to be restored relationally and to have a relationship with the church at some point. However, there are laws, issues of liability, and responsibility to protect the weak and vulnerable from people who prey upon them that will dictate what and when you can do it. I leave it to God to ultimately decide what He does with such a one; but in my humanity, it is hard for me to see how he or she could ever serve the church again in a leadership role. Churches and pastors can still engage that person with a team that will oversee them outside of church attendance if the law prohibits such attendance, and help to build bridges between them and relationships that have been broken, such as spouse and children, but not with their victims. While I believe even that relationship can and may be restored, I am not qualified to facilitate that and believe that almost no pastors are, even those who are trained counselors. The shepherd has too much responsibility to protect the sheep, so I believe he should primarily engage the repentant predator on restoration of hope and purpose for the future and leave the past to the professionals.

To be sure, I have such limited knowledge of this area that my opinion is almost inconsequential. I have met and engaged two people that fall into this category and the laws of

Tennessee made it almost impossible for them to have a relationship with the church, so I worked at just being a friend. One was a woman, so I could not befriend her at all personally. The other was a man who ultimately was looking for a next place and not a process. I cannot pretend to know his motives, but clearly, this is an area where you have to be very cautious. As an aside, consider what we create when we treat all sexual predators the same and exile them, leaving them no choice but to congregate only with other sexual predators. That looks to me like a recipe for recidivism, or a tendency to reoffend.

The Big "But"

Before we move on, let nothing I have said about restorative ministry to sexual predators be construed as defensive of their behavior or the church's indifference through the years. The victim has to be heard and protected at all costs. If both victim and predator are in your sphere of influence and one relationship or the other has to be sacrificed, err on the side of the victim. Make a phone call to a brother pastor who has a heart for restoration and hand him off to that pastor. If the predator is genuinely repentant, he or she will understand.

If you have not done so already, I encourage you to read the *Caring Well* report delivered to the Southern Baptist Convention in June of 2019.[13] In particular, I was both touched and convicted by the story of Dr. Susan Codone prior to the introduction. It is a stark reminder that not following the process legally and morally is not an option. The reminder that we are not in a Biblical position to extend

---

[13] Report from the SBC Sexual Abuse Advisory Group. https://caringwell.com/wp-content/uploads/2019/06/SBC-Caring-Well-Report-June-2019.pdf. Accessed June 18, 2020.

mercy to the predator is necessary for all of us who work in the area of restorative ministry.

Dr. Codone writes, "Sexual abuse is not a mistake, bad behavior, a reaction to stress, or a lapse in judgment. It is a crime, and abusers must face arrest and prosecution. In Southern Baptist culture, we have reversed God's design; forgiveness and mercy originate from the victim and from God, not from the church as an employer. Determining innocence or guilt belongs to the courts. Sexual abuse is sin, but in classic preaching mnemonics, the sin driving sexual abuse is empowered by our culture of Silence, Indifference, and Neglect."

To summarize, restoration of a person caught in sexual predation means helping them own it, repent of it, and move past it into a new normality that provides guard rails in the future, but it does not mean protecting them or the church.

Before You Move On

The reality is that you may never face a decision over whether or not to get involved in a restoration with someone accused of a sexual crime. Most are so ashamed they just want to hide if they are repentant, or are so self-deceived and deluded that God has given them over to a depraved mind and the last thing they want to do is come clean, pay the penalty, and start over. Chances are, though, that a substantial part of the need for restoration that will cross your path will be due to sexual failure of some kind.

It is important to note that as distasteful and potentially divisive as these situations are, we are told that we are to leave the 99 and pursue the one lost sheep that has wandered away. How much more should we seek to restore those who come to us unprompted, seeking help?

For Further Thought:

1. Have you taken the time to forge your own Biblical view of sexual sin and/or divorce and how the church should react to it? If not, spend some time differentiating between what has been passed down to you and what the Holy Scriptures say as revealed to you by the Holy Spirit.

2. Before you ever consider engaging a person accused or convicted of sexual crime, make sure you know the laws of your state, the policies of your church, and the extent of your liability insurance coverage. If you do not have written policies both to protect your members from sexual predators and yourself and your church from liability, you should probably stop here and get to work on that. Your denomination or local ministry network would be a good resource.

3. When have you seen a member or colleague fail sexually and ultimately find restoration to church and/or family? What were the support systems that you saw work for them?

cul·ture

/ˈkəlCHər/ *noun* 1. the customs, arts, social institutions, and achievements of a particular nation, people, or other social group.

Peter Drucker - "Culture eats strategy for breakfast."

Chapter 10

Developing a Restoration Culture

If I have not said it enough to this point, and as if I won't say it a few more times, let me point out this is hard work. It is made hard by the pain of all parties involved, and made even harder when the church family has a history of disposing of people rather than restoring them. That happens so easily for a number of reasons, and we will discuss some of them; but without a healthy church culture that is bent toward loving broken people and is willing to be made uncomfortable by sinful people, it will be very hard to become a safe place of restoration. As a pastor or church leader, you need to have a good handle on the climate and culture of your church as it relates to restoration before you take on a person and engage them in a process.

If a pastor in your community is caught embezzling money from the church and approaches you, asking if he and his wife can attend your church while they try to pick up the broken pieces of their life, what would you say or do? Do you know how your leaders and faithful attenders would react to sitting on a pew with the pastor who is on the nightly news during his trial? What about the youth minister that has a sexual relationship with a 19 year old college girl he first met when she was in his youth group? Though it may not be illegal in your state, how would your church feel about that young man sitting in your building week after week? What if a member of your church has an affair and causes a divorce before coming to his senses and wants to find his way back to God, even though his wife has not forgiven him?

I am not saying all these people should be in your church, and circumstances might make it impossible. Ask yourself, "Is the default position of our congregation a warm and welcoming place for broken people, or is there an unwritten rule that 'we like people who have it all together?'" I was once told by an older colleague that I should never ask a question in a business meeting if I did not know the answer beforehand. I am still a little unsure of that advice, but I am sure you need to know the answer to this question before you get blindsided.

Every pastor I know is of the opinion that his church is friendly, warm, and welcoming. I fall in that category myself. I have been in some of those churches that bragged about how friendly they were and felt like an outsider, too. In church revitalization, we are often told that people are not looking for a friendly church, they are looking for a friend.

Honestly, though, restorative ministry needs more than just a willingness to nod and make a seat for new people. It is not just being friendly. There needs to be a deep love for the broken and battered that only comes from the Holy Spirit. It means a church has to have a different attitude about church than most people in first world countries do today. It means that they are not only accepting, but like Paul, are willing to struggle to see Christ fully formed in those that come (Galatians 4:19).

It means being a place where broken people can be appropriately transparent about their failure and know there will be loving accountability and support. It means having a church that trusts its leaders enough to know they are involved in a messy situation with someone without having to know the details. It means being a church that will go the extra mile to help someone practically who is in the worst season of her life, whether that is a community job search, relocation assistance, financial help, or babysitting.

Essentially, restoration is incubated best in a culture of people that can love people and not label them by their failure. You will know you are getting there when your people become more proud of who they have aided than they are of the sterling reputation of their congregation.

That kind of culture does not happen by accident and rarely happens without dedicated leadership pulling them in that direction. A church is almost never all accepting or all opposed to restorative ministry and it rocks back and forth along the continuum, depending on recent results and their evaluation of those results. We will talk about some things leadership can do to keep the soil of restoration healthy in a moment, but first, let's acknowledge that there will be opposition.

The Pushback

Let's return to Luke 15 and be reminded that there were three main characters in the story we know as the prodigal son. We love the picture of the repentant son who has come to his senses and is walking toward home rehearsing the speech he is going to make to his father, a speech he never gets to fully give. We also love the picture of God in the waiting and expectant father who sees his son from a great distance, then runs to him and loves him and celebrates his return. We can see the parallels of both of these characters in the ministry of restoration.

For some in our church, if they could have a moment of candor, they would most clearly identify with the older brother. He heard the party sounds but was in no mood to party. As far as he was concerned, the younger brother had already gotten his fair share, while he stayed home to care for dad and run the farm and had received no reward for it. Most people in our churches don't think out loud about the broken, expressing opinions such as, "They deserve what they got," or "They made their bed, let them lie in it." Some do resent the fact that the pastor and leaders are spending time and resources on a guy who created his own crisis, when the pastor could be doing something more productive. Perhaps he should be witnessing to that man at work whose name the church member had given him instead of witnessing to the man themselves. It really comes down to self-righteousness for those who truly have the older brother mentality. They think to themselves, "I stayed home and did the right thing. Why should he be rewarded for messing up so badly?"

Not all those who are uneasy with restorative ministry in your congregation are self-righteous. Some are genuinely fearful. Some have deeply rooted theological and traditional ideas they cannot shake, and believe that to practice restoration is wrong in certain instances. Others have spent a lifetime carefully guarding the reputation of their church and are really concerned about what their friends in the community might think, especially if the person being restored offended at that friend's church.

There is something really scary about inviting in people who are already messed up into our relatively sterile and safe church environment. It is also hard for people to forgive those former leaders who hurt them or their church. For some reason, it is most difficult to forgive and restore those we actually know. You might have some personal reluctance or encounter some concern from some well-meaning board members or lay leaders over the relatively low return on investment. After all, if you succeed, they probably won't remain here in our church, and most of the time it does not work anyway.

Restoration is sometimes easier in theory than in practice. To be sure, there are some people who are just hard hearted toward the broken, often because they have never suffered brokenness in their own life to date; but they are few and far between. Most can be led to understand the value and necessity of restorative ministry, given good leadership.

Before we talk about four tools you can use to develop that culture in your church, let me point out that new churches and recovering churches are more easily led in this direction. That does not mean those established and plateaued churches cannot move toward restoration, it is just easier in places that are not as solidified. We will deal with some of that in the next chapter.

Tool #1: Preaching

I can almost hear the audible sigh of relief. Preaching is most often our favorite tool for fixing anything. Typically, we are better at it than anything else we do. Teddy Roosevelt spoke of his "bully pulpit," and you have one, too. Yes, it is a sacred place, and it is God's property; but He has entrusted it to you and called you to be their pastor-teacher. For some of you, you are not the lead pastor, but you are a leader in the church. Use your influence and whatever platform God has given you to influence your church family toward restoration.

It has been said in the church world for years that the most powerful place of promotion is the pulpit, and the most powerful person of promotion is the pastor. If the Father has placed you there and put restorative ministry on your heart, use that powerful place of promotion to call your church to love God and love those whom God loves, even those who smell like they just woke up in a pig pen. When you come to the Word of God with restoration on your heart, you will see it on almost every page of Scripture. You don't even have to preach sermons entirely about restoration, just point out as it comes up in your text all the places God is restoring people and all the ways He calls us to join Him in that work. I struggle to remember ever preaching a full sermon specifically about the ministry of restoration at our church, but it has become part of the vernacular.

These are some of my favorite Bible passages that teach restorative ministry principles. Isaiah 42 prophesies of a coming Messiah that does not throw people away. It was such a powerful statement that Jesus repeated it in Matthew 12:20. "A bruised reed He will not break, and a smoldering wick he will not quench." In the last hours of Jesus' life on earth, Peter denied him three times and cursed aloud. What do you think your board would do if this Sunday you denied knowing Jesus and used profanity? Do you think there might be a called meeting that afternoon? Jesus took that guy and built the church on his little statement of faith! That same Peter, based on personal experience, gave us 1 Peter 5:10: "And after you have suffered a little while, the God of all grace, who has called you to his eternal glory in Christ, will himself restore, confirm, strengthen, and establish you." Don't forget that Jonah got a second chance, and basically blew it, too, but God still used him. David committed the most widely known sexual sin in the history of Christianity, then had a man killed to cover it up. The book of Acts tells us that he "fulfilled the purposes of God in his lifetime." To be certain, he and his family paid a price, but God restored him.

My African friend and interpreter, Patrick Kiseli, often gets so amused at my southern colloquialisms that he laughs so hard, he cannot interpret. Once, I was preaching and said that when the only tool you have is a hammer, everything looks like a nail. He just kind of stared at me, but you know what I mean. If restoration is on your heart, it will come out in your preaching. Commit in your own heart to be the one that does not snuff out a smoldering believer and does not discard a bruised believer, and then preach it. Entrust those seeds of God to bear fruit and not return to you void.

Tool #2: Modeling

You don't have to wait for your church to be fully committed to the ministry of healing and restoration before you get involved. You might get an organic opportunity to do so by simply being available to an old friend or colleague. The secret to modeling restoration for your people is to understand the appropriate level of information they need. You don't want to unnecessarily air anyone's dirty laundry, but let your people know there is a process of covenant restoration going on as a part of the church's outreach, and that you are involved. It is difficult at the very beginning because the church leaders and members may have no frame of reference, and those fears and concerns we discussed earlier can be almost paralytic.

As time goes on, you will have some stories to tell them. Those might be just stories of incremental steps someone is in the process of taking. They might not even know the person or the situation, but you can let them know it is happening and God is working. I am a big believer in celebrating the little wins. Look for ways to help your church celebrate when they get to be involved in God's work of restoration. Storytelling and personal testimonies that speak specifically to how God has used you and/or individuals in the church to bring about restoration tills the soil for future seeds of restoration. In short, your church needs to see you practicing restoration ministry and not just preaching it. When you love the messy, it gives unspoken permission for your members to love them as well, and to proactively seek them out. When your church members decide by watching you that it is OK for their friends to not be OK, opportunities for restoration will begin to multiply.

Tool #3: Coaching

As I said earlier, you can expect opposition. Some of that opposition will be more deeply entrenched than others; and often, it will surprise you where that entrenched pushback originates. You might be surprised to hear reluctance or even what feels like antagonism from a person that has most often been on board with your vision and program. You have been able to count on them for support all along and, quite honestly, it can be baffling when they are not supportive.

I remember early in my ministry at the church I serve now a conversation with a respected elder and leader in our church at that time who questioned our outreach to some fairly messed up people. He was not rude, rebellious, or angry, but he was concerned. His specific question makes all kinds of sense in our human reasoning. He simply wanted to know how these incredibly messed up people that are so far from God are going to become the kind of people that can be healthy contributing church members in the future. His was a genuine concern for the future of the church, and he spoke like a true business professional when he questioned if the return on investment was too small long term to see the church regain its footing. Thankfully, several years later, we have seen the opposite prove to be true.

You cannot coach everyone in your church to bring them on board, but you do need to recognize the gatekeepers and spend some time helping them get on board. You can do that by providing books like this for them to read. A good way to do that is to say "I have been reading this book about the church and its role in healing broken church leaders. I feel we need to be doing more of that. Would you be willing to read this and then have a conversation with me about it? I want to make sure I am hearing from God and not missing anything here."

Coaching is also accomplished when you take some key leaders into your confidence and ask them to be part of a restoration team for an individual. The first one should be an easy win for them, perhaps someone from outside their circle of influence that is in need of help. It is often easier to get started with someone you don't know than with someone who hurt others in your sphere. Later in the book, you will hear of the importance of having different kinds of people on each restoration team, including some whose judgment you trust, even if they do not know the person they are helping to restore. This is another one of those "little wins" that you can celebrate. Some of your key leaders just need to see it in action.

Tool #4: Mentoring

Mentoring and coaching are different in one respect. Coaches are almost always on the sideline and are always involved in the game planning and execution. Mentors pour into individuals regularly but do not necessarily hover near, choosing instead to release them to do the work and just use you as an advisor.

So much of what we do in church work makes people think the elders or pastors always have to take the lead. A great way to create a culture of restoration is to help some of your men and women lead some restoration teams of their own. Maybe a church member has a friend that has had a major upheaval in their life and find themselves in need of restoration. If they are talking to the member about it, maybe that member should lead the process instead of you. You can meet with the member regularly to debrief, offer encouragement, advise, and support, but that member has the ultimate responsibility for that team and that process.

It might be hard to get everyone in the decision making process to sign on initially to your desire to create a culture where restoration is the norm rather than the exception. The more people you coach and release to actually do the work of restoration, the more the culture will develop.

Culture Killers

You will find that not only is it true that not everyone gets on board, but it is also true that not everyone stays on board. It is a culture that has to be constantly monitored, maintained, and motivated. Even with wins under the belt, people will grow complacent or get frustrated and say "why bother?"

People will get frustrated because broken people are, well... BROKEN! Broken people, even restored broken people, have some baggage that can sometimes make it hard to love them. Perhaps you have never pondered this, but do you suppose that the prodigal son never did anything to disappoint the father and anger the older brother again? Assuming he was not perfect from that point on, can you imagine people might have rolled their eyes and said, "Here we go again!" That will happen in your church. Even when a brother or sister has been restored, they will make mistakes and may even re-offend. In a culture with a history of being judgmental, it will be easy to slip back into some old patterns and want to insulate against both failure and disappointment.

In the years since this turned into the covenant process that we practice today, we have had badly broken people that bailed on the process early because a church was willing to take a chance on them. Literally, to do that, they broke their promise to us; it was disappointing. Others said they trusted us but when the covenant was presented, they pushed back and refused to commit. Some signed on and just drug their feet about meetings, counseling appointments, and assignments. Others have been impatient, pushing for a quick resolution and a rubber stamp that says they are cured or restored. All of these things will cause the church to wonder if it is indeed worth it. That is why it is so critical to celebrate the wins and continue to coach, preach, mentor, and model the process of restoration.

Before You Move On

Some churches need to not only talk about it informally, but officially adopt a process of restoration as a church that will come into play when a leader or member suffers a public failure of some kind. It can be as simple as a statement that your church is committed to restoring people through a covenant process, or as wide as naming an official church restoration team and leader through your deacon or elder process. Being sure restoration is discussed in both the formal and informal church conversations keeps the culture receptive to hurting people and makes sure you are ready when the need happens. Anything short of a culture of restoration will make success highly unlikely.

For Further Thought:

1. Who are people of peace from the core of your church who lean toward restorative ministry? What can you do to fan the flame for them?

2. When was the last time you preached a sermon or series on the role of restoration in the church? Is there a date or season on your upcoming preaching calendar that you could use to till the soil of culture change in this area?

3. Does your church currently have a bent toward healing and restoration? Is there a process in place that is clearly defined? If so, outline it here. If not, take a few minutes to organize your thoughts about what a restoration process could look like in your church.

Chapter 11

Restoration Grows Best in the Soil of Brokenness

My friend and co-author, Michael, wrote a great book a few years ago on the parable of the soils[14] that Jesus spoke in three of the synoptic gospels. In it, he fleshes out the reality that the kind of soil seed lands in has a great deal to do with the kind of fruit produced by that seed. As we try to become a "catching church" rather than a "pitching church," a place where bruised reeds are not discarded and flickering wicks are not snuffed out, we must pay careful attention to the kind of soil being developed in our own hearts, the hearts of our leaders, and the general attitude of our churches. Let Michael share some principles of dirt you need to know if you are going to develop a culture where hurting "seeds" can fall to the ground and die to be reborn healthy and useful according to John 12:24.

Principles of Dirt

In Matthew 13, Jesus taught how the hearts of people can differ regarding openness, or receptiveness, to God's Word. And He knows the true condition of our hearts, even when we don't. I (Michael) like to say that the Creator/Carpenter has the dirt on all of us! His analogy uses dirt in various conditions to represent each type of person. And we are all present in His word pictures.

In my book, I point out the basics of Jesus' parable before inviting readers to perform their own soil analysis. In

---

[14] Michael Stover, *Jesus and Dirt: A Fresh Look at the Parable of the Sower* (CreateSpace Independent Publishing, January 23, 2017).

Jesus' teaching from Matthew 13, the seed is the Word of God, the Sower is Jesus (and by extension, those who share God's Word with others), and the soil is the hearts of men and women that display different levels of receptivity. After that, the soil examination becomes more personal.

Unprepared Ground

The path ground Jesus describes are the byways left untilled between fields. In our day of mechanized, high-productivity, commercial farming, no inch of ground goes unused. In Jesus' day, fields were tilled by hand with space allowed between them for foot and animal traffic. These paths were trodden underfoot and baked by the sun until, over time, they became impenetrable. Farmers did not bother to use it, or even till this soil, so it continued to harden. When seed was scattered and some inadvertently fell on it, they bounced around and lay naked in the sunshine. Harsh heat baked these seeds and the birds eventually came and ate them.

This path ground is a word picture for men and women whose hearts have been hardened by exposure to negative elements. Trodden down by the harsh realities of life. Pummeled by coarse interactions with people. Baked and scorched by the hot, searing effects of willful disobedience.

Path ground is not only unprepared, it is unreceptive. Jesus' words in Matthew 13:19 go beyond mental comprehension to include volitional acceptance. This means the person with a heart of path ground not only doesn't understand what is heard, they do not want to hear or understand (see Zechariah 7:12). Matthew 21:33-45 is a great example. In this account the Scribes and Pharisees knew Jesus' parables were about them; they understood His teaching. And yet, they still looked for ways to arrest Him! Their heart was already hardened against anything Jesus had to say. They were prepared beforehand to reject His teaching. His words didn't change them. They couldn't penetrate.

Jesus explained that it is as if such people never heard His words at all. The enemy comes and snatches away any knowledge or memory of God's truth. Maybe you have said these words: "They've been in church all their lives. They've been exposed to bible teaching. How can they make those selfish choices?" The explanation is simple, if tragic. Such people hardened their hearts toward God's truth, refusing to receive it, and it's as if they never heard it. Some even sit through church services refusing to open their hearts to the Word of God and His work, including restoration. Their mind is made up; they already know they will make no effort to really listen, repent, and surrender.

Stoney Ground

When Jesus spoke of rocky soil, He wasn't referring to dirt filled with loose stones. He was talking about a field with a thin layer of soil hiding the bedrock underneath. When seeds fell upon those kinds of places, it burrowed down into the ground until it hit rock. The roots could go no further, so the plant immediately sprang up, because it had no depth of soil. If the roots hit bedrock and can't go down, the force of energy moves upward and the plant springs up quicker than normal. A farmer may assume this is the greatest crop yet. However, the roots desperately need water, but can't penetrate the rock to get it.

The plants looked healthy at first, but when the sun burned hot, they withered because they had no deep root to provide all that was needed. The moisture that was originally in the plant evaporated in the heat of the sun. When the roots tried to get more, there wasn't any way to go down and get it. The plant burned and died and was unproductive.

According to Jesus' explanation, these are people who showed an interest in Jesus and the Word of God. They may have been fed, healed, or otherwise served by Him. And in response to His kindness, they made a shallow, emotional response without genuine acceptance. Many are helped by the church and show an initial interest in spiritual things. But when pressure or persecution comes, or difficulties arise related to living a Kingdom lifestyle or performing the difficult work of restoration, they stumble and wither away. The problem wasn't the heat of the sun; it was the lack of life-sustaining roots. Occasional trips to church may make you feel good, but the overall problem is not being addressed: there is no rooted faith in, and commitment to, Christ.

Thorny Ground

Matthew 13:7 is the shortest line in the entire account, and yet the weeds it describes cause the most damage. The 'thorns' here are various types of weeds that spring up and choke the good seed plants. Because weeds grow higher and faster than good plants, they block out and absorb more sunlight while consuming water and nutrients the good plants need. Every gardener knows the unending battle to keep weeds from taking over and destroying everything good.

In Jesus' story, these weeds are the worries of life and the lure of wealth (vs. 22) that crowd out any time or attention given to spiritual growth or Kingdom concerns. Instead of being driven from the truth by hardship (as in the stony ground), this person is drawn away from the truth by the promise of something better.

Just like Johnson grass in your family garden, these weeds appear to be something good. Most people want to be respectable, well-to-do citizens who take good care of their families and are able to set aside money for their kids' college and nice vacations. What's wrong with that? Nothing overt.

But, because these things resemble blessings from God, we pursue them and ask God to bring them to pass as His blessing. But in our pursuit of them, we often neglect eternally-valuable matters such as discipleship, holiness, evangelism, and restoring the broken to wholeness and usefulness in the Kingdom. Our datebook and our checkbook reveal with startling clarity what is most important to us.

Good Ground

Thank you Lord Jesus for the good ground in our churches, described in Matthew 7:8, 23. This person's heart is open to receiving the seed of God's Word and displays a willingness to obey. Hearing is never enough; there must be an intent toward obedience as well (James 1:22). Due to their openness, this person puts down roots, gaining depth of understanding and resulting obedience. They actively pull weeds, removing anything that competes with loyalty to Christ. They bear fruits of holiness and righteousness from precious seed (see Matthew 7:20; John 15:5, 8).

Getting to Good Ground

Jesus made it clear that every person's spiritual heart condition is represented by one of these four types of soil. Path ground pictures hardened hearts that refuse to understand God's Word. Their minds are already made up and they are unwilling to listen or change. Stony ground pictures hearts that have shown an emotional, shallow response to the gospel. When trouble comes they stumble and wither away and bear no fruit. Thorny (weedy) ground pictures hearts that allow the concerns of this life and the pursuit of wealth to choke out the Word before it can grow and produce fruit. And, thankfully, good ground is tilled, soft, and receptive to seed that can grow and produce a bountiful harvest.

How can we cultivate hearts that resemble good ground? *Plow the soil.* Break up the hardened soil in order to receive good seed. The first step in this process is repentance. When God's Spirit makes us aware of such hardness and indifference, we must make a deliberate turn away from that path and turn toward the path leading to God. God's instructions to Israel through the prophet Hosea are the prescription that leads to good ground.

"Plant the good seeds of righteousness, and you will harvest a crop of love. Plow up the hard ground of your hearts, for now is the time to seek the Lord, that he may come and shower righteousness upon you."

Hosea 10:12 (NLT)

Broken People Living in a Broken World

Christian people seem to be bent on an eternal quest to answer the big questions of the faith, and none is bigger than the question of human suffering. We ask "why?" from an honest heart, but we do not like the answer. Why do bad things happen to good people, as though any person is really good? Why does God allow that to happen? Why does one man's sin cause another man to suffer? More personally, why would a pastor or church leader succumb to such hideous sin, and how did he or she ever think they would get away with it?

The reason we seem to be eternally asking those questions is that we don't like the simple answers that God would give. That answer requires two things that are in short supply, great faith and humility. There is a simple answer but it is hard to stomach, especially in the western church. Are you ready for it? Buckle your seat belt! This is BIG! Bad things happen and good people sin because we are broken people, living in a broken world.

That is right, I said it. WE are broken people living in a broken world. From the garden, man has been broken, but it started even before then. That brokenness is rooted in the fall of Lucifer, and his core issue is pride. The earliest we have knowledge of him, he is rallying the angels of heaven in a coup against the most loving, benevolent, and grace-filled Person in the universe. His pride made him want it all. When he was dispatched from heaven, he set his sights on God's crowning creation, mankind, and led them in pride to do the one thing God told them not to do. From that time, we understand that man is born into sin; but what we don't often process is that original sin is rooted in pride. I want. I can do it. I know better. It's all about me. There is a little "wannabe" God in all of us doing its best to get out.

Much of what happens to cause the need for restoration in the body of Christ is a direct result of pride. That individual pride often becomes corporate pride. Pastors grow proud of "my" church and boards of leaders feel led to defend "our" church. We all want people to invite their friends to church, but even that can quickly devolve into bragging about our programs and what makes ours the best church to attend.

Humanly, we can understand that we would probably not be attending the church if we had not arrived at the conclusion that it was best at something. Few people join a church based on their gifts, the needs of the community, and how God could use them in that church. Even fewer people leave a church because they are not being used effectively to lead people to Christ.

We join the church because it "meets my needs," and leave the church because "I am not being fed." These are words every pastor has heard. It is a tension we wrestle with — wanting our parishioners to love and believe in the church where we serve, but fearing the pride that comes with it.

139

The problem with this is that the prouder a church gets of its staff, its programs, its buildings, and its reputation, the harder it is to be a place where messy people can be loved, nurtured, and restored. The more we buy into the idea of putting our pastor on a pedestal, the easier it is to put our church and ourselves on a pedestal. When that happens, a messed up, fallen church member or, God forbid, a broken and messed up pastor or staff member or elder, is summarily tossed away because it mars our understanding of what our church is and is supposed to look like. A church with that kind of thinking is a church whose soil would reject the idea of restoration and where weeds of distrust and judgment would choke out the ministry of healing.

In Matthew 23:25-28, Jesus addressed the Pharisees as he often did and specifically taught them about what goes wrong when pride goes to church. We would do well to learn from it before a church member, a colleague, or a staff member needs the church to have soil that can grow a ministry that reconciles and restores rather than discards.

I remember when I finished my restoration process, the church where I had served held a going away reception for me. In responding to a comment, I told a member how grateful I was for their grace-filled approach. That member replied, "We were able to do that because you taught us how." Even that statement reeks of pride, but it underlines the need to constantly be preparing and challenging your congregation in the area of pride. Jesus never missed an opportunity to gouge the leaders of the synagogues about their pride and hypocrisy. We can learn from His teaching what makes it so hard for a church or leaders to cultivate a soil that admits our own brokenness, so that broken people feel safe submitting to a restoration process in our church.

Looking Good is More Important than Being Good

In Matthew 23:28, Jesus says, "You outwardly appear righteous but inside you are full of hypocrisy and lawlessness." It reminds me of a childhood commercial for Starkist Tuna where Charley Tuna, a cartoon character, was always trying to impress people, The tagline was that Starkist wanted tuna that tastes good, not tuna with good taste. Somehow the pharisees, the religious leaders of the day, misunderstood that God was far more interested in who they were, rather than who they appeared to be.

Joseph Kennedy, patriarch of the political Kennedy dynasty, is quoted as telling his ambitious sons, "You must remember. It is not what you are that counts, but what people think you are." That kind of thinking worked for them and unfortunately over the years has invaded the church. The problem with that kind of thinking is that when pride goes to church, it will force broken people to live a double life.

If you are not yet convinced that all of us are broken people, there is not much I can do to convince you. We have all sinned and fall short of the glory of God (Romans 3:23), and there really is not one of us righteous, not even one (Romans 3:10). When I issue a particularly difficult altar call, I will often acknowledge the fear people have of responding, lest someone think they are a sinner. My usual line is "Let me clear that up for you — you are a sinner, I am a sinner, we are all sinners." Andy Stanley famously said, "We don't like to say we are sinners, preferring to be known as mistakers."[15] It is far easier to say, "I made a mistake," than to say, "I sinned

---

[15] Spoken in a sermon by Andy Stanley on SermonCentral.com website. https://www.sermoncentral.com/sermons/it-s-no-mistake-andy-stanley-sermon-on-salvation-139280?page=2&wc=800 Accessed June 18, 2020.

against God, the church, and my family." We need to be honest with ourselves. In many churches, we cannot admit we are sinful people, broken and in need of healing, so it becomes very difficult to offer that to others who we see as more messed up than us.

In that soil, filled with pride and maintained by proud people, there are only two choices for a person who comes to grips with his brokenness. He has to leave the church and go find someplace where they will love him through his brokenness, or he has to stay there and pretend to be as "alright" as everyone else is pretending to be. That soil leads to disposal, destruction, and death.

In Matthew, Jesus used a couple of analogies about the person who is consumed with spiritual pride — a person who washes the cup but leaves the crusty remains on the inside; and the person who makes the tomb pretty, not realizing it is full of death. In John 12:43, John describes the pharisees with the words of Isaiah, saying "For they loved the glory that comes from man more than the glory that comes from God." This is the problem of a church that is too proud to admit its own brokenness or love someone else through theirs.

He used hypocrite, a carefully chosen Greek word that Jesus plucked from the culture of the day that meant an actor who plays a role. When we play the role of a believer for an audience made up of fellow members and other churches, instead of playing to the audience of One, it becomes almost impossible to admit our failure and tolerate failure in others. In Luke 12:1, Jesus warned against the leaven, or the sin, of the pharisees, which is hypocrisy. Hypocrisy is pretending to be something you are not. Pride keeps us from admitting our need, seeking help, humbling ourselves, and repenting. Instead, we continue to go to church with the besetting sins of our lives killing us every day, more concerned about looking good to the church and community than looking real to God.

It is a dangerous condition for the true believer, because it reinforces the great Kingdom of I. It happens automatically after a while: it substitutes false spirituality for authentic relationship, it breeds self-deception, it hinders the convicting Spirit of God, it fosters fear of man rather than fear of God, and it magnifies the immediate at the expense of eternal consequences.

Here is the takeaway the Pharisees just couldn't grasp. We are not spiritually right based on anyone's opinion other than God's. Jesus, in his scathing indictment of the seven churches of Asia minor, said in Revelation 2:23, "And all the churches will know that I am he who searches mind and heart, and I will give to each of you according to your works." Hebrews 4:12-13 reads, "For the word of God is living and active, sharper than any two-edged sword, piercing to the division of soul and of spirit, of joints and of marrow, and discerning the thoughts and intentions of the heart. And no creature is hidden from his sight, but all are naked and exposed to the eyes of him to whom we must give account."

You may successfully look spiritual and hide your sin from family, church, and even self, but with surgical precision, God dissects your life and knows when in your pride, you refuse to submit and repent and instead, wash the outside of your spiritual cup.

Proud Churches Have a Misplaced Focus

In Matthew 23:23, the Lord offers another indictment we would do well to learn from. He said, "You tithe of the tiniest herbs and spices, legalistically giving a tenth of every little thing but fail to follow the great command — love God and love others." What they were doing was not wrong, but it was not enough. They were focused on the secondary issues of the law, but leaving out the biggest things like caring for the poor, acting with justice, and being faithful to God. He uses another analogy that was even stronger — straining at gnats and swallowing camels. Both gnats and camels are unclean to the Jew. When they drank wine, they would sip it through their teeth so as to strain the gnats out. He said, tongue in cheek, you do that and then swallow a camel, which is bigger and even more unclean.

It is the modern-day equivalent of arrogant Christians who never sign up to serve the poor or fight for justice, yet want to spend all their time arguing over obscure doctrines. It is when pride makes you more determined to prove you are right than to do right. Don't get me wrong. There are some tenets of the faith that are worth defending. In fact, Jude tells us in verse three to contend for those faith doctrines that are essential. But spiritual pride will lead you to get mad and defensive if people don't agree with you on every point of doctrine, and care not one whit about the broken brothers and sisters around you.

This misplaced focus will allow churches to stay very busy in endless Bible studies, while ignoring the needs of people that are different from them. Unfortunately, once a person's hidden sin becomes hidden no more, a proud church struggles to love them as Jesus taught because it reminds church members of how easily that could happen to them.

Churches that are inwardly focused are rarely restoring churches. If there is a preponderance of talk about my preferences, whether it be about music style, color of the carpet, type of homily, or anything else, there is usually little concern for broken people. The people are too busy tithing of the tiniest herb to care about the needs of messy people.

A Passion for Position

Jesus's final dig toward the pharisees in Matthew 23:6 is more personal than church focused. He said the Pharisees had developed more concern for what people thought of them, where they sat at the festivals and how people greeted them, than they were about His true mission. Here is the sad reality. Pride makes it easy to get caught up in looking spiritual, but at its extremes causes you to want others to recognize you as spiritual. He said of the spiritually proud that they enlarged their displays, they wanted the best seats, and they wanted people to recognize their importance.

You may think that will never be you, but consider how widespread it became among the early believers. Even as they witnessed Jesus condemning the Pharisees for it, it was so deeply rooted in them they did not recognize it when it came out in the open. In Matthew 18:3-4, the disciples seemed more worried about who would be greatest in the Kingdom than the mission at hand. In Mark 9:35, while walking to Capernaum, they argued among themselves about who was the greatest. HIS DISCIPLES! In Matthew 10:22, the mother of James and John, the sons of thunder, asked for her boys to be seated on each side of Jesus when he gets into His Kingdom. In Luke 22:24 , at the Last Supper, with Jesus' life on the line, the disciples come back one more time to say, "Oh, by the way, hate you have to die and all that, but we are still wondering, 'When they write a book about us, who do you think they will say is the greatest and most spiritual, hypothetically of course?'"

Here is the thing: pride is so insidious and so destructive to the life of a believer, that it makes you do stupid things. It would be funny if it were not so dangerous; but it happens all the time. You see it often in church staff and even among lay people in growing churches. We work hard and want to be recognized for our position. You see it among megachurch and non-denominational, but it is becoming more prevalent among main-line denominations to see new titles like apostle, bishop, presiding bishop, and others. There is nothing wrong with those titles, but it is really easy to have people think the best about you when you occupy a position.

That personal pride can make you concerned about who you allow to be part of your church, and selective about those with whom you are willing to be seen. Restoration requires you to be friends, and be genuinely concerned about people that most, if not all, the Christ followers you know have long ago given up on. Restoration begins with friendship. If you can't be friends with someone who is messed up, even at a level of sin from which you genuinely have never been tempted, the soil in your heart will not grow healing and restoration. It is almost a cliché by this point to say that Jesus really preferred hanging out with badly messed up people who knew they were messed up, more than He liked to socialize with the broken who not only do not know they are broken, but go to great lengths to live a double life so no one else will know they are broken.

Time to Start Plowing

Have you let yourself fall into one of these traps? Has your church fallen into the trap of looking good at the expense of living out God's goodness? Has it lost the focus Christ wants it to have on loving the least, the last, and the lost? Have you personally gotten caught up in a position or the esteem in which your church is held in the community?

Many years ago, a lady in his church told a pastor friend that their church had devolved into a "rescue mission and a psychiatric hospital!" My friend just said "thank you." Clearly that was not the answer she was looking for, but he saw it as a compliment. C.T. Studd said "Some want to live within the sound of church or chapel bell; I want to run a rescue shop within a yard of hell."[16] I am convinced that most leaders, especially those reading this book, want to develop a culture where broken people can thrive and be healed; but most are also hampered by soil that is not quite ready for that kind of seed. They are left asking, "What can I do?"

In Hosea 10:12, we are given a word picture about soil that we can use if we need to work on the soil of brokenness in our congregations. It says "Sow for yourselves righteousness; reap steadfast love; break up your fallow ground, for it is the time to seek the LORD, that he may come and rain righteousness upon you." We are told to break up the fallow ground. Into our dilemma of proud churches and proud people who struggle to love broken people, we can simply start to break up the fallow ground. In other words, the soil may be rocky, thorny, or hard, but it is time to start plowing.

I grew up on a sharecroppers farm in West Tennessee, and though I got away from farming as fast as God would let me, I learned some things about preparing the soil. Ironically, though I hated getting dirt under my fingernails, I was on a high school soil judging team. Doesn't that sound exciting? One thing I do remember from all that was how in those river bottoms, the flooding and winter would make the top layer of soil very hard. Before you could disk it or sow it, you had to plow it. I was amazed at how hard the topsoil could become in such a short period of time, but how rich it could be when the plow turned it over.

Before You Move On

If your heart is turned toward restorative ministry, maybe because of a calling or a need among the people you love, but

---

[16] Missionary Portal – Biography of C.T. Studd. http://missionaryportal.webflow.io/biography/ct-studd. Accessed June 18, 2020.

you recognize that the soil of your church is not ready for that kind of seed, you need to start plowing. You start by taking a long look at your own heart and asking God if your self-righteousness is hidden even from you, but your heart is hard toward colleagues and brothers who have engaged in sin and/or been fired by someone else who was in sin. Perhaps you have said to them, "I am praying for you," but never prayed for them. Maybe you said call me if you need me, but have not given them a second thought since. Breaking up the fallow ground in your own heart begins with repenting from a lack of concern for fellow pilgrims who have experienced an earthquake for whatever reason. It continues with your actions and your leadership. If you want to lead your church to be good soil for healing ministry, it will have to be demonstrated for your people more than anything else. Let them see you caring for people, going the extra mile, even to the point of them wondering why you don't just give up on that guy or gal. Once you have repented, and you are living out restorative ministry, you can cultivate the soil of brokenness in your people by being appropriately transparent with your own struggles, and telling stories, with permission, of those whom you are restoring.

One of the most ironic days of my ministry came on a Sunday when I was greeting people at the door. A long-time church member spoke to me on the way out, saying, "Pastor I am uncomfortable with how transparent you were in the sermon today." A few minutes later, a guest spoke to me and said, "Thank you for being vulnerable and transparent today. I thought I was the only person dealing with that." When you let people know you are not OK, it gives them permission not to be OK, and frees them from the necessity of living a double life. Nothing lets the air out of pride and develops the soil of brokenness like letting yourself and others be honest about your struggles.

For Further Thought:

1. What is your honest appraisal of the soil of your own heart today as it relates to restorative ministry? Are you comfortable enough with your own brokenness and the journey you are on to be transparent with self and others for the greater good?

2. Does the church you serve or lead have a pedestal mentality about either their leaders or the church itself or both? What causes you to feel that way?

3. Is there someone in your church family or who used to attend that has been cut off from the fellowship of the church family due to a sinful condition, a divorce, a crime? What can you do for that person today to begin to demonstrate restoration and cultivate the soil of brokenness?

Chapter 12

Culture Produces Commitment

I spend a lot of time with the students in our church family for many reasons, not the least of which is because I am an old youth pastor at heart; and I read a few years ago that one of the statistical reasons teens stay in church after high school graduation is that they have a relationship with the lead pastor. Toward that goal, I co-lead a discipling group of high school students on Sunday nights. It is a group that requires some commitment, including focus and homework, but they keep coming.

Occasionally, one of them or a former member of the group will tell me of a relationship that is developing or already underway and caution me not to tell their parents. I quickly remind them that I love them and will do what is best even if they do not like it, but then strongly encourage them to go public. After all, if you really believe this is the right thing and God's will, you will want to let people know.

In the same way, if you as a pastor or church leader have a heart for restoration, and you are leading your church to become a culture that loves the broken and to serve as soil that will nourish the broken, at some point in time, you need to go public with it. This is where well-meaning churches have failed to be places of restoration in the past. Even if the church is a loving place and the people are geared toward authentic and transparent relationships, if the church does not have a stated desire and policy to restore rather than discard people, there will be times when people in your community need help or people in your church foul up, and the pain of it will be so great, no one will just naturally be drawn toward restoration. There is value in cultivating an atmosphere and reputation as a church that historically and purposefully chooses restoration over kicking those who are down.

Restorative ministry really is a matter of the heart, and it requires a great deal of trust between pastors/leaders and the people they shepherd. Once your heart is right, it is time to move on toward the practical and the procedural. In just a few more pages, we will dig into a model you can use as a starting point to develop your own process that is unique to your environment. Before you jump to that, let's talk about how to create a public commitment to being a church and leader that restores the broken.

First Things First

I won't rehash all that we have talked about to this point, but PLEASE resist the urge to jump to public commitment first before you have done the hard work of deciding if you want to lead this kind of messy ministry, and deciding if you are personally ready to take on such a task. Take the time to be sure your church is healthy. Do what Scripture teaches us in Luke 14:28-30: count the cost. Restoration at its core is a matter of the heart. What do you believe about fallen comrades? Do you believe the grace of God is sufficient to rescue the alcoholic pastor who is shamed publicly when he gets a DUI charge?

What does your church think about the pastor who has a surgery and gets addicted to pain pills so badly that he gets caught stealing them from a parishioner's medicine cabinet? Does your theology allow for grace to the young staff member who does not get caught but goes public with his lifetime struggle with same-sex attraction, and admits he has been seeing someone secretly? If and when, and I mean only if and only when, you are convinced that God wants you to be a person of grace toward the broken believer, and when you believe your church is both healthy enough and aware of the needs, then you are ready to say, "we want to be a place of restoration."

Counting the cost means understanding there are colleagues and community members who will not agree with you. It means that you are willing to open your heart and your church to someone who is likely to disappoint you and may in fact, reoffend. Counting the cost means you understand the double edged sword of Galatians 6:1, that we are to restore the fallen, but be aware of the sins involved that may also attack you. Failure is not contagious, but we all face a common enemy of the soul. Genesis 4:7 reminds us that if we do not do well, "sin is crouching at the door and its desire is contrary to you." An eyes-open approach is acknowledging all the ways this can go sideways, yet still believing God has called you to join Him in the great work of restoring believers.

Making a commitment to moving forward involves an honest understanding of the level of trust between pastor and people and both sides being committed not to breach that trust while choosing to be OK with much of the ministry of restoration taking place behind closed doors. Years ago, I was working with a young man on a church staff who had been caught stealing from another person in the church. I remember a woman who was uninvolved in either the problem or the solution cornering me and demanding to know what he did to get fired and why we did not put him in jail. She said with a toss of her head and a stomp of her foot, "I am a member and I have a right to know." In even the healthiest of churches, you are going to have people who feel that way, but it cannot be many of them. I told her firmly that she was not involved, and in fact, did NOT have a right to know.

Even among believers there is a certain amount of schadenfreude. That is a word of Dutch and German origin that means to take pleasure that is derived from another's misfortune. You get a little picture of that in the heart of almost every man when you get in a traffic jam for an hour just to finally get past it and find out nothing happened on your side of the interstate, the jam was caused by people slowing down to look at the wreck on the other side. We all just kind of like to be in the know.

The kind of trust that is comfortable with you or someone else inviting broken people into your fellowship has to begin at the top. You must trust your systems and not do anything to go around the systems, even for a professional colleague. Sometimes, we think we are doing him or her a favor by keeping it secret instead of letting people know that person needs a specific kind of help for a specific kind of reason. Dr. Bob Jones, Sr., is quoted as the originator of this statement. "It is never right to do wrong in order to do right."[17] Building trust with your people means always doing the right thing in the right way. If you can't do it that way, your church is not ready to embrace restoration ministry.

Partnership

In essence, what we are talking about here is a church-based plan and process for restoration. Even if your church is not on board, you can be part of restoring broken people. It would just be very hard to be the point person if your church is not in agreement, and especially if it is someone who has sinned against your church.

I will return to two different stories from earlier in the book. I told you about one of my older members who when I told some former members that Antioch had become a place of restoration, quickly chimed in that it was more about

---

[17] Heard numerous times by the author, as quoted by his pastor. Anecdotal.

Pastor Pete than Antioch. I began the book with Dr. Jess Moody's statement that some churches are pitchers and some are catchers and "we want to be catchers." The first statement underlines a failing of our early days of restorative ministry at Antioch. I assumed it should be private, quiet, under the radar. Much of it still has to be; but when I compared us to Dr. Moody's church, I realized that although I wanted to be a catcher, I was not trusting my church to decide for themselves that they wanted to be catchers, too.

All of us know that churches take on the personality of long tenured pastors. But my not giving them a voice and a choice to wholeheartedly join me in this journey was not fair to them, and caused me to miss out on a lot of resources that could be tapped for healing and restoration. In the days since we went public, we have found hurting people places to stay, jobs, accountability partners, and more, that I would never have known about had Antioch not bought into the process. At the same time, I have discovered that the more secret your sin remains, the greater hold Satan has on you.

Proverbs 28:13 admonishes that "Whoever conceals his transgression will not prosper, but he who confesses and forsakes them will obtain mercy." When a church is safe for people to not be OK, it gives them courage to face the future without hiding out in their shame. Furthermore, the more public a person is with their failure, the more likely they are to have friendships and resources that will keep them from doing the same thing again. Be a partner with your people, and be loud and proud about it.

Oh, THAT thing!

This part is so insignificant in the greater scheme of things and your church may have no history to overcome, so feel free to skip this session if all is good. However, in the quest to develop a culture of restoration and partnership with your people to bring about restoration, there is one more thing I learned completely by accident. The church I serve now and where restoration is a way of life has not always been that way. They have always been a more loving church than any I have ever served, but for whatever reason, they had a long list of former pastors and staff members who had left under less than ideal circumstances. Even some long-tenured pastors and staff members left disillusioned and discouraged. Many of the relationships were strained, and as is often the case, when someone or a group found one thing they did not like about a former leader, they forgot all the good they had done.

When I became the pastor, I began to systematically bring back former pastors and staff members to preach and fellowship with us. I did not realize at the time what I was doing. I believed then and believe now that I was simply hearing and obeying God as we tried to turn around a trend of years of decline at the church. An unexpected byproduct of that was one of the first high-profile restorations of our ministry, when a pastor I told you about earlier came back to apologize to the church and wound up staying. He is still on my staff and handles all the pastoral care visits now to some of the very people that forced his resignation nearly 30 years ago.

If the church you serve has one or several former pastors who left under duress or wounded the church badly, it is probably going to be necessary for the church and you to find a way to build a bridge to that former pastor. Remember again, restoration is not putting things back like they were, nor is it telling someone what they did was OK. It is building bridges over which a newer normal can be established. If a church does not believe their former leader or pastor is worthy of their forgiveness, acceptance, and resources, it will be hard for them to have any credibility with anyone else. When I have been called on to mediate conversations between churches and former leaders, I can almost see the ice melt when I tell them that Richard who was fired is back on our team 30 years later.

I would suggest a brief history review with some people you trust who have been around a long time. Recognize that even those who are loving and kind will see the problem event through their own bias, so don't worry too much about their evaluation. You are really just looking for the facts. How many former members and staff have been ignored or pushed away when either they did something illegal, immoral, or unethical, OR they did something the power structure did not like? Just make a list of the names and start the process of getting to know them. Not everyone will be glad to hear from you, and the church will not be glad to hear from all of them. You will need to be careful who you let engage the church after all this time, and what pace you want to do it. There will be some deeply wounded family members who are still in the church, and some deeply wounded members who either feel their pastor/friend was mistreated or they were mistreated by that pastor or staff member.

It took me nearly two years to get six people back in front of the church. One was a staff member who "planted" a church, but the perception was that he took people from the church while they were struggling and because they did not make him the pastor. Another was a man they really loved but were disappointed, as he was given great latitude to finish his doctorate and left quickly afterward. Another was a layman who had led large Sunday School classes and mission trips and then flamed out, leaving his family. There were several more, but you get the picture. Not all were bad guys, but there was unfinished business and both people and churches with unfinished business can have short fuses. The last thing you want to have when dealing with people in need of restoration is impatience.

156

A counselor friend constantly reminds me that in the behavioral health world, the mantra is that "the best predictor of future behavior is past behavior."[18] If your church has a long history of discarding people who disappoint them, it will be very hard for them to restore others who have disappointed them and their loved ones. I know nothing about the little church body that my friend went to after being fired by his church. He went on a Sunday night and worshipped with a ministry colleague who sadly had to inform him on that Tuesday that his members did not want that broken pastor back. They were friends with people in the church that fired him. That is just to remind us that culture almost always wins out over desire. Make sure the church has done the right thing in the past or is at least willing to make amends now.

For many churches, the first step is simply acknowledging there is a string of broken relationships that have never been resolved and becoming willing to make amends if possible. Almost all 12-step groups have a step in the healing process that goes something like this. "I made a list of all those who I offended and became willing to make amends to those people, so long as doing so would not cause them further harm." Churches, like people, cannot always make amends. Some of those relationships may have become so toxic that the person cannot even be contacted. Others may have died. Yet, when it can be done, it makes a huge difference, both to that person and to the church.

My first church job was at University Parkway Baptist Church in Johnson City, Tennessee. It had once been a thriving church led by an articulate, young, prematurely silver-haired man. Over the years, a power struggle developed between him and some families in the church. Back then, I

---

[18] Attributed by the author to Regina Harrell, Licensed Professional Counselor, Johnson City, Tennessee.

could tell you who was right or wrong; but as the years have gone by, I have come to realize there are two sides to every story, and only a fool makes up his or her mind after hearing only one side of the story.

At some point, the power struggle came to an end. The pastor was gone. Whether he was fired or resigned is a matter of debate to this day. The church was a shell of its former self and that pastor's family was deeply wounded. There was a whole generation of key families who were forever lost to the Kingdom. They were meeting with 40-50 people in a room that would seat 600 when they called another pastor.

I was long gone when all that happened. From a distance, I heard about a day when the church came to a place of repentance and invited that pastor back and loved him, encouraged him, and had him to preach. He has been dead now for several years, but his son is a member of the church I currently serve and has often told me how much that meant to him and his family. In fact, the granddaughter and great granddaughter of the old pastor are active in that church to this day, and the church is healthy and vibrant and reaching a new generation. They have done a lot of things right, but I am convinced a significant part of their rebirth was making amends to that pastor.

Finally, Something We Can Do

Once the past is evaluated and is in process of being put to rest, you can move on to one of the steps in the process of restoration. Even if you are not completely finished with those past issues, once you have notched some little wins, you can begin the process of formulating a simple statement of intent to be a church where broken people, even those who are broken in that church, will find a process of healing and hope. It does not need to be wordy. In fact, I think brief is better. It does need to say in some way that the intention of this church is to be a place where broken people will be loved, accepted, and nurtured. It can be something as simple as this:

It is the intention of XYZ Church, led by the Holy Spirit, to engage in a ministry of restoring broken leaders and members of the body of Christ, whether in this local body or another. We are committed to providing a process, leadership, and resources to assist the broken in finding their way back to spiritual wholeness. We are committed to being a place where broken people will find love, acceptance, and accountability, because our Lord has shown that same love and acceptance to us.

There is value in preaching the need and the reason for such a statement, and then working it through your church decision-making systems toward a final vote. When I make that statement, most people push back, asking if all churches are not supposed to do that anyway. Of course they are, but most do not. If you aim at nothing, you will hit it every time. Having a statement of intent on file, and perhaps even posted somewhere, gives you authority when a deacon has an affair and is repentant, but his friends in the church are so disappointed they just want him gone. It also points out that it is not just about saying a broken person is OK and welcome, but it acknowledges that it would be unloving to let them remain the way they are, and therefore provides a process to help them toward healing and restoration. What you are really doing is declaring intent in advance so that when a decision needs to be made, it is not made on the basis of personality or level of pain, but is driven by vision and commitment.

Guarding the Trust

In restoration ministry, you need to know there are some lines you just cannot cross and maintain the trust of your people. I have already talked to you about sex offenders and some of the needs that have come up along that line. Some of those I have just been able to befriend, but not engage with any of the resources of Antioch Church. Others, I have just had to be honest and share that I simply did not have the bandwidth to help them at that time.

I am predisposed toward helping everyone and can easily get in over my head. This is another value to having your church leadership in on the decision-making from the very beginning. We also know that not everyone who says they are repentant are truly ready to have those conversations. In fact, they may still be cycling through sinful seasons and could become predatory in the church. This is not just true of sexual predators; there are other predators as well. People who sin financially will move on from church to church to find other marks, or more commonly, because they are users and have used up all the resources where they were. Just recently, we have had to say no to a church family whom we had helped financially dozens of times. They were not changing their habits or actions at all but continuing to depend on us to bail them out. It does not mean they are not loved, but just that they are not ready for restoration. Just like in benevolence, having a team of people takes the load off of just one person, and also gives the added benefit of more wisdom.

When the church knows you not only know where the lines are, but receive and value input when you don't, their trust in you will grow. With the benefit of added trust comes more expansive ministry opportunities. We are ministering to people right now that we could not have taken on five years ago because we have guarded the trust of the congregation.

Before You Move On

This is a very small piece of the puzzle, but from experience, we know that there is balance to restorative ministry. Every church's balance is different, so there is no set number I can give you. I *can* tell you that it takes healthy sheep to restore unhealthy sheep. Churches that get so many unhealthy sheep in the flock that it overwhelms the organization and process find themselves losing healthy sheep. A surface evaluation might lead us to believe those departing healthy sheep left because they did not like the unhealthy sheep being around. While that can be true, most often it starts to happen because the system was collapsing under its own weight. There is no limit to the number of broken and de-churched people in your community, but as my Executive Pastor, Aaron Cox, is prone to say, "Not every small group meeting can be a 12-step meeting." If that becomes all that your church does, you will have difficulty attracting and retaining healthy sheep. They will just wear out and move on. Let your leadership help you work on balance if like me, you have a hard time saying no.

Each church is different and most churches won't ever get close to that line. In fact, some of you reading this are just interested in how to help one person, not creating a culture that attracts broken people. There is nothing wrong with that; but if you are drawn toward hurting people, pay attention to how weary your healthy members get, and take your foot off the gas pedal occasionally.

My friends, Pastor Scott Parker and his wife, Nikki, have built an entire ministry at By His Blood Church that is focused on reaching and restoring the broken. Most of their flock is either in recovery or moving that way. Many are homeless or recently homeless. Yet, even the Parkers recognize the need for boundaries. Guard the trust of your church and protect the healthy sheep, even as you develop a church culture of love and restoration for the unhealthy.

For Further Thought:

1. What is the trust meter reading between you and your people? Do you trust them to follow you into unknown places? Do they trust you not to lead them into danger? What do you think would be the reaction if you asked them to formally commit to pursuing broken people?

2. Has your church adopted a policy toward those who sin against the church and/or publicly fail? If not, do you think you are ready? What work needs to be done to get ready?

3. When have you experienced ministry imbalance with more needs than healthy people to meet those needs? Is the balance good in your church today?

Chapter 13

Restorative Ministry is Kingdom-Sized

There are some of you who picked this book up because you know someone who is hurting badly and in need of someone to help them. It might be a seminary colleague, a former staff member or elder, or just someone you know in the community. They are your friend and they need help and you want to help them; and I have spent all this time talking about need and culture. You are thinking, enough already. This paralysis of analysis is killing me. Just show me the process.

Others of you also know someone like those above and you have been reading all this and thinking that your friend needs help and you want to help them — but after reading all this, you are suffering from the paralysis of analysis and think, "I don't have what it takes. I am not equipped for this. My church is not ready, either — spiritually or culturally — to take this on; so what does that mean? Does my friend just have to suffer because I am not ready and my church is not ready?"

I know of almost no church and pastor that is completely ready and resourced to step into restoration ministry. Even if they have most of the puzzle pieces in place, it is such a time-consuming ministry, almost no one has the time to do it alone. On the other hand, I have never met a pastor who had a heart for restorative ministry that did not have some of the pieces already in place, and who could not start doing something, even if they were not ready to do everything. That goes for lay leaders and churches as well.

Kingdom Networks

I have a quirky, theological bent toward the idea of a local church. Every time the New Testament refers to a local church, it does not speak of a subnamed church, such as First Baptist or Covenant Presbyterian. Instead, it speaks of the church at a geographical location, such as the church at Philadelphia, or the Church at Corinth, or the Church at Thessalonica. I am convinced there were many smaller subgroups of most of those geographical churches, but it appears to me that God sees us as one body. Imagine that!

I think that is still true today. Within a stone's throw of Antioch Church where I serve is Midway, Greenwood, Southside, and Grace Fellowship Churches. Each of us have our own unique personality, demographic, style, and calling, but all of us are the Church at Johnson City, in God's eyes. I sort of think of the ones that meet with me as the house groups of the early church. Again, I am not saying that is mainstream thinking, but it drives what I am about to tell you.

Chances are that your church does not have everything they need to restore a broken brother, but you have something to bring to the table. There may be other pastors who serve alongside you who God has not urged toward restorative ministry, but in the words of Henry Blackaby, they would like to join God where He is at work.[19] They may not have a friend in trouble and they may not be as invested as you are, but most share a Kingdom mindset and would be willing to help where they can. They have some unique resources that are available to you through networking.

---

[19] Henry Blackaby, Richard Blackaby, Claude King, *Experiencing God – Knowing and Doing the Will of God* (B&H Publishing, September 1, 2008).

I serve on the board of a non-profit homeless ministry in our community and the Executive Director[20] uses an acronym that I had never heard before hearing it from him. It is OPM, and it is short for "other people's money." He is always talking about the importance of using every resource available; so if another non-profit, NGO, or grant-funded organization can help us meet the needs of one of our clients, why not spend OPM? Money is tight in churches, but there are skills, buildings, people, and more that can be leveraged in an effort to help broken people get back on their feet. We will call it OPR, "other people's resources."

So far, in this journey of helping people get back on their feet after an earthquake of some kind, I have never done so without the help of someone from another church, or without tapping into the resources of another church. Sometimes, it looks like calling on a pastor who has no idea of how to do restorative ministry and coaching him to lead the process, since the broken person is a close friend of that pastor. Other times, the failure is of such a specific type of sin that no one in my circle is qualified to have the conversation. Those times I have called around to ask other pastors and lay leaders who they knew that had expertise in that area. Almost always, there are relationships in that person's life that need to be addressed by someone other than me. I have a couple of pastor's wives, other than my own, who have suffered through similar crises, and exited it in a good place both spiritually and relationally, who are willing to befriend a bewildered and pain-wracked wife whose husband has suffered an earthquake.

You don't know OPR is available until you need it. However, you have to be cultivating relationships with other pastors and ministries before you need it or you won't know

---

[20] Bob Hall, Executive Director of Family Promise of Greater Johnson City.

where to look. This is another negative side effect of our "lone ranger" approach to ministry. We get too busy building our own church to have those life-giving relationships that protect us from an earthquake; but we also are so isolated that we do not know who or what outside our church can be used to minister to hurting people.

People of Peace

Some of the most significant OPRs out there are pastors who are wired to love hurting people. We know that some pastors are more people-driven than others. They are the ones who get their hands dirty in local benevolence in hopes of seeing life change in the recipients. They are the ones who enjoy the hospital visits and love the personal interaction. A subset of those pastors is a group of guys who are aware of the needs of the pastors in their community and in their network, and both pray for them and keep in touch with them to encourage them. In the vernacular of missions, these pastors are people of peace toward restoration. My friend, Jerry Jeter,[21] has a list of pastors he prays for regularly and lets them know via text and social media that he is thinking of them. My church is 300 miles from his, but he still prays for me. Locally, Pastor Greg Burton[22] is one of those guys who not only prays for local pastors, but visits them in the hospital or at the funeral home in times of grief. These are the kind of pastors of peace you will need to identify if you need to restore a fallen leader.

You will need to identify and cultivate relationships with these pastors because there will be times when your plate is full, and you need to hand off a broken and battered brother or sister to someone who has more bandwidth than you at the moment. Other times, you will need their advice, need

---

[21] Rev. Jerry Jeter, Pleasant View Baptist Church, Clarksville, TN.
[22] Dr. Greg Burton, Colonial Heights Baptist Church, Kingsport, TN.

access to experts in their church, or quite honestly, may need their help paying for professional counseling.

A few times, we have encountered a pastor who had been fired, either for cause or just because he was not a right fit and the situation was not handled right. Having lived in the pastorium of the small church, these typically younger pastors or staff members have not only lost their job, but they have lost their home. So often, like my co-author Michael, their only choice is to move back home to parents or move in with friends. At the same time, most established pastors learned long ago they need to buy their own home. Many of those churches have sold the houses, but many have not. It has been a great joy to help network needs and resources together to allow a pastor to move his family into an unused parsonage to allow time for job search and healing. Two unintended consequences of that arrangement have been a blessing.

First, the hosting church has found themselves energized by the opportunity to love a hurting pastor as small groups and other subsets have reached out to their new tenants. For the typically older churches that are usually the ones that held onto the houses, those young pastor families bring a breath of fresh air to their congregation.

A second blessing is that the pastor is wired to serve and often brings skills and gifts to the church that blesses them even as he and his family are blessed. We do not have a large pool of these stories, but the ones that happened saw the person being restored use his handiwork ability to fix up the parsonage and work on the church. After a few months, one minister with permission of his restoration team began to make hospital visits to assist the pastor and felt like he was giving something back.

The only way that will work is when you also bring your resources to the table. It may not be in the area of restorative ministry, but the only way networking works is for all of us to do what we can do individually and trust God to provide our unmet needs through Kingdom contacts. For us, we have a small bucket of money that can be used for professional counseling if needed and have offered that to other churches. We have some professional counselors in our church who have made themselves available outside office hours to meet with people, and we routinely help them network with other pastors to help hurting people.

Safe Haven Churches

If your church is ready to love people who may have made some really big mistakes that have gone public, you are in a position to offer one of the most valuable resources there is — that of a safe haven for the broken and their family. In retrospect, the hardest part of my journey after I flamed ten years ago was reconnecting with a local church. I never had to look for a church before, and honestly, did not know how. Multiply that with the shame, loss of identity, and sense of failure that I felt, and you get an idea how hard it is to find a church. Without Pastor Rick White and The People's Church reaching out to me the way they did, I might have continued to worship in anonymity and never plugged into a local church.

Just being accepting of those who are broken does not make a safe haven. You as a leader and the church in general have to pursue the broken. It does not matter what happened to you or what you did, if you are broken, you walk around with a whisper from the enemy in your mind that you are not good enough and that you have failed. You think everybody knows and because everybody knows, no one will want you. Safe haven churches have to bend over backwards to let broken people know they are loved and wanted.

Safe haven churches are necessary because often, the ones who have offended cannot stay in the same church; it is just too hard on the ones who have been hurt. It is not necessarily unforgiveness on their part, but in the early stages, when the pain is most acute, just seeing the offender is too painful. At the same time, in those early days, if there is not a safe haven for the offender, he will drift further and further from restoration, convinced that he will never recover. Truthfully, because some don't find that safe haven, they find solid ground in their family and seek another career, but are never restored to a healthy relationship with the church.

I can name dozens of former ministers that I am friends with today who have never successfully reintegrated with church. There are lots of side effects to that, but I think the worst of them is the generational effect it has on that pastor's family.

My friend, Sammy, was associate pastor of a church that fired him over something that happened in his extended family. Clearly there are two sides to that story, but Sammy eventually joined my church after ten years away from church. He and his wife have struggled with depression and related illness, and at this time, neither he, his children, or his grandchildren have been able to put down roots in a local church.

I am convinced, based on what happened in my life, that the reason I am not in the same position was the church that became a safe haven for me. My community group never questioned me about what happened, they just loved me. After a few months, I found myself laughing again and enjoying church life. For so many I have met that did not have that, they feel guilty and try to make themselves go to church, but laughter and enjoyment are the last words they would use to describe their relationship with the church.

Some of those safe haven churches are drawn to particular kinds of brokenness. There is nothing wrong with that. You don't have to be good at everything. Remember, this is a Kingdom endeavor. If you do what you are good at, you can trust God to raise up someone else to do the parts that you cannot do.

Restoration Specialists

In the past few years, I have developed a list of resources that names churches and pastors who are willing to help, but it also includes some special people who through their own brokenness or a special calling have devoted their lives to caring for hurting leaders in the church. A pastor who wants to be a facilitator of restoration needs to continually build and strengthen his network.

Some of these specialists are preventive. Hearken back to my story. I knew several months before my crash that I was in trouble and reached out to some people I had heard of, only to find out that help was inaccessible to me. Shortly afterward, though, I began to realize there was an entire network of unsung heroes who work to understand, support, encourage, and empower pastors and church leaders so they do not blow up or blow out. These organizations, like SHOR (Shepherd's Haven of Rest) headquartered in Memphis and Energize Ministries based in NC, are national in their reach. They offer preventive care to pastors and church leaders in hopes of avoiding the need for restoration. Not every person you talk to will need to be restored if you can connect them with help before something bad happens. That is just two of many, but I was ignorant of the Kingdom resources that I could have tapped into instead of sinking further into depression and pain.

Other specialists are craftsmen who have a unique ability to help a person find their way back after an earthquake.

When my pastor emeritus was serving on my restoration team, he made an observation that I have thought of many times. He said that you can tell what is happening on a job site by the type of tools they are using. Demolition is done with big, heavy, hard-hitting tools like wrecking balls and bulldozers. If you see those in front of an old building, you know it is coming down. If the purpose is restoration, the tools are smaller, more specialized, and uniquely suited to the job. Organizations like FIG Ministries and Restoration Inn and the folks at First Baptist of Woodstock, Georgia's City of Refuge use those specialized tools to help restore broken people.

In addition to those national ministries, I have discovered there are pastors and retreat directors and counselors in local ministries all around us who are focused on a particular kind of need and will be glad to help you. It is both a practical and Biblical imperative that you get to know them so that restoration can happen. Remember that restoration is a team sport, and that team does not all have to come from within your organization. We are part of a greater KINGDOM!

Before You Move On

Before you can network Kingdom partners in a process of restorative ministry, you have to be a Kingdom partner yourself in other areas. You don't have to participate in everything available in your local area, but if you never partner with another church and you never sacrifice anything to see their ministry grow, it will be nearly impossible to get them to share with you unless they are predisposed that way. Find a way to selflessly interact with others in the Kingdom BEFORE you need them.

For Further Thought:

1. What are some resources you think your church or small group can bring to the table to assist in the process of restoration? What are your church's strengths?

2. Who can you identify among local pastors and churches that share your heart for restoration? What churches do you know of in your area that have a reputation of being particularly accepting of people who have suffered earthquakes?

3. Do you know any restoration specialists, either nationally or locally, that you can call on if needed? List them here.

Proc·ess

ˈpräˌses,ˈprōˌses/ *noun* 1. a series of actions or steps taken in order to achieve a particular end.

"For which of you, desiring to build a tower, does not first sit down and count the cost, whether he has enough to complete it?" Luke 14:28

"And I am sure of this, that he who began a good work in you will bring it to completion at the day of Jesus Christ." Philippians 1:6

Chapter 14

Process Matters & Restoration is in the Details

Congratulations on getting to this point in the book. Many of you who just have a friend or church member in need of restoration have picked it up and skipped right to this section. I don't blame you. I would, too. I would encourage you when the immediate need is over and you have understood and implemented a process for your friend, to go back and read some of the rest of the book. Right now, you are in no mood to start a restorative ministry or develop a restoration ministry and culture in your church. You are just trying to figure out how to help someone. If that is you, you have come to the right place. For those of you who have read the whole thing, thanks. That continues to surprise me.

In this final section of the book, we are going to talk about a little more than just restoration as theory and culture, but begin talking about a process. It is a process built around a covenant agreement between the person in need of restoration and the team/church that has agreed to oversee his or her restoration. It is detailed and will require effort on the part of both parties. We will discuss the why's of that later, but this final section of the book will be wrapped around the idea of this covenant and the details of formalizing and implementing this agreement.

As a young preacher, I was given a book of sermons[23] by Dr. Jack Hyles. While my ministry and style could not be further from his either in scope or style, I was struck by his love for the hurting and his love for the Bible. One of those sermons was called "Don't Rush the Washing Machine." In

---

[23] Jack Hyles, *Grace & Truth Book of Sermons* (Hyles-Anderson Publishing, 1975). Chapter 2.

it, he discussed the value of each cycle of a washing machine, and the importance to the end product of clean laundry of keeping those cycles in order. He said that spinning is important, but spinning without first rinsing and washing has no value. The covenant process keeps the cycles of restoration in order, because each step is important to the end product.

Details Matter

Most people who first come to the table with us in restoration, both those who are in need and the team offering the help, find the covenant to be too much. Typically, the first conversations we have are about why we need all the steps. Let me pause here and say that as you get into a process-driven restoration, you will learn that not all the steps are always necessary for every person; but on the front end, it is helpful to have them in writing. For a person who is desperate to get back to a normal life and at times, a ministry job, there is a desire to move fast — to rush the washing machine. While I was not really thinking of returning to ministry, I was in a hurry to put this episode behind me, and at times, I really chaffed under the nuance and detail.

The covenant process, established up front, made me have some conversations that, had they not occurred, I may have found myself back in that same pit. I recognize things in myself to this day and I am able to avoid those pits simply because the covenant process, led by a Godly and discerning team, made me slow down and dig deeper. I remember in particular being angry when they pushed back after reading something I had written as an assignment, and they did not feel, or at least implied they did not feel, that I was being transparent. Yet, those difficult meetings pushed me deeper into personal and spiritual evaluation that revealed things to me I did not know about myself. Having a baseline, covenant process and some people on the team who won't be pushed toward shortcuts is essential to true, Biblical restoration.

The Danger of Good Intentions

The rest of this book will be built around the covenant restoration process and the value of its steps in helping a person reconnect with self, family, friends, and perhaps, ministry. This process is really where the rubber meets the road. Few people are willing to follow it; interestingly enough, even churches that love broken people are reluctant to hold a person accountable to a process. That may be due to time constraints or the difficulty of holding a friend or colleague accountable. It sometimes feels like you are kicking a man when he is down. Nothing could be further from the truth, but feelings are feelings. When you are on the receiving end of restoration, you tend to feel everybody is judging you, and now, the people that are supposed to be helping you are adding to that chorus of judgment.

The process is valuable because it requires effort, introspection, hard work, commitment, and engagement from the team, the restoree, and ultimately, the church. People who suffer earthquakes, like myself, tend to have a narrow view of what happened, seeing it as an isolated event, rather than the culmination of a lot of little events along the way. The commitment of the restoree to that hard work, especially the introspection it requires, is often what reveals the core issues that led to the earthquake. If you don't get to the fault line we discussed earlier, and assist that person in building structures in his or her life that will stand firm against the next earthquake, you are just setting them up for further failure.

How many famous Christian leaders do you know who have suffered an earthquake event and hurried back toward vocational ministry, only to re-offend later? Yet, others who quietly took what they had coming and left the limelight for a season were able to resume ministry at a different place or level and were effective for many years.

The old adage says, "the road to hell is paved with good intentions." Just being a friend and cultivating a safe haven culture for people in need of restoration is just good intentions without a process in place. That is where most pastors and churches that really love people and have a heart for those whom everyone else have given up on really struggle. They have a tendency to love the broken but shake their heads sadly, believing that they will never be useful in leadership again; or they just welcome the person into their fellowship and let them hang around a while without doing anything to help them get back in the saddle. After a few months or even years, the broken person gets back to serving somewhere, but is a candidate to suffer another failure because they were never given a process that required them to understand what had happened and how they could avoid it in the future. A church or leadership team that has a process in place in addition to those good intentions, is the church that is really prepared to help someone move past their past into a new future.

It avoids the road that is paved with good intentions where churches develop a culture of love for the broken, but just welcome them into the church family and either never allow them to work themselves back to a place of service and influence, OR they just let them hang around a while and then put them back to work. That person often is still beset by the same issues that led to their first downfall and are in a precarious position of potentially falling again. There is a huge difference between being a church that loves people and being a church that loves people enough to help them deal with the issues in their lives in order to bring restoration.

The Exception to the Rule

Not every broken person you encounter will need a formal process of restoration. As we have developed this process, we have met several people who, unlike me, were self-aware enough to see that they were about to become unraveled. They also knew that if they continued down the path they were on, they were going to suffer an earthquake that would cause great pain, not only to them but to the people they serve and the people they love. These brave folks confessed up front what was eating them from the inside and the sins that were starting to become strongholds in their lives. Because they had not failed publicly and had not crossed a line, they did not need restoration. They needed to repent and get some help, perhaps counseling or accountability, but they had not ripped apart significant relationships in their sin, so there was no need to restore those things. We offered assistance and encouragement, but it was an entirely different type of ministry than what we are talking about here.

Those in Need

So many, though, like me, do need a formal process, because their failure is public. Without a formal process that provides a ramp back into the significant relationships of their lives, such as family, friends, colleagues, and ministry partners, they will often feel useless, isolated, and have no hope of ever returning to any level of spiritual normalcy. A restoration process is necessary for those who have broken rules of the organizations they serve, rendering them disqualified, have crossed Biblical boundaries, sinned in public, committed a crime, broken their ministry or marriage vows, or otherwise had a public failure. There are times when a person whose sin has not risen to disqualification, and who has not crossed a line that caused public reproach or embarrassment, needs a restorative process. If he is repentant and wants to remove the stinger of Satan who might wait until a more opportune time to reveal that sin, it may be advisable to go through a public season of restoration and healing. I told you earlier about the itinerant speaker friend who was not sinning, and had not given in to any temptations, but he was just running on empty. That person may not need the whole shooting match, but at least needs a team to help him figure out where the disconnect happened.

The Value of Process

It is in the process that both the offenders and the offended can have honest, meaningful conversations without being accusing or defensive. It is in those conversations with a team of caring, restoring brothers or sisters that a person can examine themselves and the series of events that led them to the place they are without feeling like they are under attack. It is a place where people they have wounded can have their pain validated and hopefully feel restored to a new place of love and respect for the restoree. It is the place where, with supervision, amends can be made and new relationship models can be developed.

The process also provides a way for a person who has suffered an earthquake to face the future. Inevitably, every Christian leader who has ever failed, whether it is in marriage, management, or personally, and then returns to using his or her gifts to serve the Lord, will have to answer some questions from people who were not involved in the process and were not hurt by their failure. Though it happens less frequently these days, I still have some people question my qualification to serve God either as a pastor, writer, or speaker. The ones with an honest heart will ask me directly, and I don't worry much about the rest. When they are honest enough to say something like, "Wait a minute! Aren't you that preacher that blew up a few years ago in Middle Tennessee?" I can honestly say two things. First, I always say, "Yes, that was me, and let me tell you about a process that I went through to deal with the aftermath of that event." Then I give them the names and numbers of the men who walked through that with me as part of the restoration team.

There is great value for the future of anyone who has been sidelined in being able to say "Yes, that was me, but I have done the hard work of getting back to where I am today, and I am willing to tell you anything you need to know. I wish it had not happened, but God is using it in my life and ministry today." The only way that happens is if a clear process led by trustworthy people is in place and followed.

A Helicopter View

What follows is an overview of the various components that we have found to be necessary parts of a healthy restoration process. In the chapters to come, we will flesh them out in detail. For now, just see the big picture and try not to be overwhelmed. The value is in the journey, not trying to check things off the list. We will give you later an actual sample restoration covenant agreement, so do not worry about trying to see how this all fits together here.

The Covenant — It does not matter which comes first, but every successful restoration process that we have experienced involved the covenant and the restoration team. The covenant is actually a formalized document that the members of the team and the candidate for restoration sign in a commitment to the process. It outlines the expectations of both the team and the restoree, as well as outlines what the process can and cannot do. It never guarantees a return to vocational ministry or even to family restoration, but provides a roadmap that allows the Holy Spirit to do the work of restoring those relationships.

The Restoration Team — As we continue, we will talk about the way a restoration team is developed and the reasons for it. Here, note the importance of having a team made up of people who care deeply about the broken brother. The team is typically chosen by the church or leader who the restoree has enlisted to assist them, with input from both the candidate and the church, plus the injured ones in his orbit. It rarely includes the injured parties, but their input is needed because if there is to be restoration, the injured parties have to believe in the team's commitment to transparency and real healing, not just in word only.

The Accountability Team — Different from the restoration team, the accountability team is selected completely by the candidate and gives him a place where he can be completely honest and open about current struggles in his life. When a person is pursuing restoration and has voluntarily submitted to the oversight of a team, it might be hard for him to admit he needs help with a particular fault line out of fear of slowing down the process. At times, he will need to vent some frustration toward the restoration team, and this team gives him a safe place to do that. Additionally, it begins to build into his lifestyle honest accountability, which may not have been present during the runup to his failure.

Journal — There will be a great deal of writing and taking notes during the process, and a journal is recommended. The candidate will keep notes and record his feelings and reactions to each of the team meetings, answers to questions posed by the team, prayer needs, fears, lessons learned, and more.

Church Attendance — We have already discussed how hard it is for former staff members and pastors or even lay leaders to attend church when they have failed while serving in a leadership role. It is made even more difficult if they are clergy, as they typically don't make decisions about church attendance the way laity do. A significant piece of the restoration process is the accountability and assistance of the restoration team in finding the restoree a place to worship where he or she can grow and be nurtured during this timeout.

Counseling — Few people who suffer spiritual earthquakes in their lives do so out of outright rebellion and a dogged insistence on doing the wrong thing, even when they know it will hurt them and others. We have discussed cause, fault, sin, and earthquakes in other places, but let it suffice to say here that most people who face earthquakes have hidden fault lines in their lives that may even be hidden from themselves. Counseling is needed in a majority of cases to help them discover the needs and build structures to keep those fault lines from creating future earthquakes. The restoration team may need to help discern what type of counseling is needed and provide funding to help meet that need. Counseling is often necessary for those around the broken restoree, such as spouse, children, and others.

Introspective Writing

As each of these components are being implemented, there are several steps in the process that require the candidate to put some things in writing that are painful but necessary. There is a step in the process that we will discuss soon that requires a written confession that is not too graphic, but is specific about what the restoree did wrong and how they found themselves willing to do that. To a person, everyone I have walked through this process with says those written documents are the most painful part of the process. However, they have later confided in me that putting some things in writing made them face things they would never have otherwise. Personally, ten years past the process, I still go back and look over those documents when I feel distant in my relationship with God or overwhelmed by my ministry responsibilities. It gives me a good reminder of where I will wind up without dedicated self and soul care.

I recommend that each restoree keep those documents in a secure location, either in a notebook or in a secure computer file. They are a record of your spiritual journey during a difficult season. One day, he or she can look back at that season and be grateful for all God taught them in the process and how far they have come.

Before You Move On

Probably the most difficult "aha" moment of the process for a broken brother or sister is that realization that this is going to take a while. If a person has made their living as a staff member or pastor and has not had a "real" job in many years, they are filled with fear and want to rush the process to get a rubber stamp from someone who will say they are ok, restored, and usable for ministry. I have said from the beginning that this process is not about giving a guy a pass to go back to work, but is a plan to build bridges to restore significant relationships; and if it leads to future vocational ministry, so be it. For many pastors/staff members, it is unthinkable that they can't get back to work in the field they have trained for and the only thing they know.

As an aside, being told to seek secular employment by my team and being assisted by them in finding a job was one of the most beneficial parts of the process. Working in a secular job allowed me to be "just" a church member and feel no compulsion to hide my weaknesses or cover up my past. I could just be another broken guy going to church and letting God slowly heal me.

Now, don't hear me say I liked it. I did not. I chafed under the authority of people who had once walked under my spiritual authority. For one full year, I did not have their

183

permission to preach, teach, or pray in public. I was told to sit and learn and listen and hear what God had for me. On one occasion, I was asked to preach the funeral of a friend's mother, but after consulting with my team, had to tell the friend I could not do it. I did not fully understand then, and may not understand all that even now, but there was a hidden arrogance that had grown in me, and perhaps in some or all of us who lead people spiritually. Letting someone else tell me what to do did not come easily, but I know now I needed that season.

Like everyone else, I was in a hurry. My life was in shambles. My family needed me to make more money than an entry level employee. Yet, I learned then and I have seen in many cases of restoration since then, that in the words of Jack Hyles, you cannot rush the washing machine.[24] A restoration process is a crock pot, not a microwave. The value of the process, unrushed by a need for religious employment, is kind of like slow cooking — it tenderizes the soul and allows the injured time to heal.

Rushing through the process minimizes the self-awareness that can only be gained via long, thoughtful conversations and introspection. Being in a hurry also makes those who have been wounded question both the validity of the process and the results. Knowing someone spent time working through the things that led them to that earthquake opens the door to healing relationships that cannot happen in a lightning process.

For Further Thought:

1. In your years of faith and leadership, where have you seen or experienced poor results because you or someone else did

---

[24] Ibid.

not follow the process?

2. Let's take your pulse currently on the process of restoration. As you look at the different areas and components, are you resistant to the detail, willing but overwhelmed, glad to have a track to run on, etc.? Why do you feel that way?

3. Have you seen people who have experienced earthquakes that did not take the time to work through a process of healing? If so, what have you observed? Has it been long enough to determine if they have found real healing and hope?

Chapter 15

Restorative Ministry is a Team Sport

Restoration is an extremely personal but not necessarily private process for the leader or layperson who has found themselves shipwrecked. By that, I mean that restoration efforts most often take place under the radar, without the knowledge or involvement of the general church public.

Yet, it has been our experience that one-on-one restoration is rarely effective. In fact, in our collective experience, small as it may be, we have never seen anyone who wanted to go through the process of restoration with only the help of a life coach, mentor, or counselor succeed.

Remember, restoration is not only the work of the Spirit in the life of the person who has fallen, offended, or been wounded. It is also the work of the Spirit in the life of those who were wounded or offended by the person and in the relationships between them. For that reason, it appears the most effective model of restoration is a team model.

None of that is to discredit the work of coaches, mentors, or counselors in the process. In fact, as we flesh out the process in the next chapters, you will see all of those things covered in the covenant. But as stand-alones, they are incomplete in their ability to do the full work of restoration. A mentor or coach may be seen as only concerned about the restoree at the expense of the church or family that has been wounded in his crisis. A counselor might be very helpful to the broken in learning how to cope with their new reality, but have no standing in helping the ripples of relationships that have also been affected.

The other reality of restorative ministry is that it is exhausting, especially if it becomes a way of life for a church or leader. If you or your organization become known as a place of healing and help, people will find you and God will use you in this vital work.

When a pastor/leader tries to do it on their own for a long period of time, they, too, suffer burnout and become a sitting duck for a cataclysmic event of their own. It does not matter how strong your counseling and encouraging gifts are, if the load gets heavy enough, and the journey is long enough, those gifts can become the seeds of your own destruction. We all need traveling partners in every ministry, and no place is that more necessary than in restorative ministry.

Team Selection

There may well be a team of the deacons/elders in a church that have a general overview of major restoration processes underway in the church; but there needs to be a specific team that is agreed upon by the church (whoever speaks for the church in that situation - for us it is now the leadership team rather than the entire church) and the individual in need of restoration. The size of the team is not significant, although it can get too large and unwieldy pretty quickly. The largest we have ever used is five people plus the restoree and the pastor/leader. Think of the difficulty of scheduling with that seven, much less more than that. Most often, we work with just three plus the restoree and team leader. When I (Pete) went through the restoration process, there were four plus myself for a total of five that had to coordinate times and places.

The team is made up of people who are selected for both what they bring to the table and for who they are in the life of the restoree and the respect they hold in the eyes of the churches involved in the process. One member of the team is selected by the restoree with the approval of the process leader, simply because the process is long, painful, and at times tedious. He or she needs a friend who is predisposed to being on his or her side. The only input the leader or the rest of the team has into that selection is an instance when that person seems to be unable to integrate into the team and process and wants to short circuit the process because of their friendship with the person being restored. We have never had to exercise a veto over that selection, but we do reserve the right to do so.

The balance of the team is selected by the leader of the process or by the church acting through their established leadership selection process. In our organization, either the person who is leading the process or the pastor selects the team and approaches them individually. Even then, the needs of the restoree are taken into account. It is counterproductive for the team to be made up of people who are inclined toward harshness or have been so hurt by the individual that they want to exact a pound of flesh. It is equally counterproductive to have people on the team who are inclined to rubber stamp a quick and easy process that will neither work toward health for the individual nor forgiveness from the former church or ministry the restoree led.

It is helpful to have people on the team who know the person well; but we have also found that as the number of people in need of restoration has increased and people have migrated toward our process, that it is sometimes impossible to have people like that available for local meetings. In that case, we reach out to people who, although they do not know the person involved, have a heart for broken people, a deep commitment to Biblical standards, and a heart that is tuned toward mercy. Those with strong prophetic gifts are not usually good choices because they can seem harsh; and those who are off the chart in mercy gifts typically have a hard time being tough when toughness is required.

Once you have settled on the people to ask, you need to make sure they have the time and spiritual and emotional bandwidth to engage in such a process. There are not a lot of meetings. Typically the team will meet monthly, although often more frequently in the early stages of the process. However, there is much time devoted to prayer, encouragement, and even evaluation between meetings. It is hard to underestimate the spiritual pushback of an enemy of our soul who feels as though the person you are restoring is already his. When you start trying to take ground from the enemy that he thinks is already under his control, the level of attack gets intense quickly. The person choosing to join the team needs to do so with eyes wide open, and those selecting them need to be confident they have the foundation to withstand such an attack.

One recent team was made up of myself (Pete), the restoree, a former business partner of his, a deacon from the church that knew him when he was actively serving God, and a friend he selected. My personal team years ago was made up of the pastor emeritus, executive pastor, and deacon chairman of the church where I crashed, plus our local Director of Missions. Another recent process involving a pastor who had an affair with a member of the church was led by me and joined by his first pastor, his childhood youth pastor, and a respected pastor in our community.

Team Responsibilities

From the very beginning, the responsibilities and goals of both the team and the restoree need to be fully understood by everyone involved. This is the reason for the Restoration Covenant that will be covered in a subsequent chapter. Several people, both on the teams and those in need of restoration, have balked at the prospect of signing the covenant. But we never proceed until they are ready to do that because it outlines expectations and goals of everyone

189

involved. As each process unfolds, there are additional steps in the process that arise, OR we discover that one step in the process is unnecessary in this instance. Regardless, the covenant gives us a baseline for the responsibilities of all parties.

The primary responsibility of the team is to be prayerfully committed to the overall process that will restore significant relationships that have been severed and restore purpose to the restoree in their Christian journey. As I have said before, it is not necessarily restoration to vocational ministry; the goal is restoration to spiritual and relational health and stability and to give the restoree a foundation on which to build new relationships, both with friends and family and with ministry organizations. (At this stage in the journey, I have dozens of healthy relationships with people I let down many years ago because of the careful work of my team.)

That responsibility requires some members of the team to listen to the broken hearts of wives who have been abandoned, children who have been betrayed, churches who have been let down, or staff members that have been deceived. It often requires the team member to discern between two wildly divergent accounts of the same situation and be able to discern and push back if necessary. This part of the process means a team member may have to be the one that says now is not the time or there is nothing you can do to bring that relationship back to health. That does not mean it is hopeless; but it means the person being restored does not have the standing or ability to instigate it. The team member who has to get involved in these discussions does not make that decision unilaterally but brings it to the team for further conversation.

As an aside, most 12-step recovery groups have a saying in their meetings that "addicts tend to disclose too much too early in an effort to cleanse their conscience and unnecessarily hurt others while relieving their own guilt." While we are rarely dealing with addicts, it is also true in restoration. The restoree wants to get on with his or her life and wants to move too quickly at times, failing to give those damaged in the wake of the crisis the necessary time to heal and deal. The team becomes the governor on that process.

The Restoration Team administers the covenant process and the pace, reviewing documents, providing accountability to ensure the process is entered into sincerely and thoroughly. When a person's livelihood is involved, even if they don't mean to, they can "phone in" the process unless there is accountability. A careful and prayerful oversight team will ask timely and probing questions, push back when something is being glossed over, and require time to soak in what is being learned.

As the process unfolds, the team serves as liaisons between the stakeholders such as the former church, family members, current church, etc. They decide when apologies should be offered, both public and written, and when the restoree is ready to exercise his spiritual gifts in the place he is currently attending. It will be up to the team when the restoree is ready to resume public ministry. That does not mean they cannot and should not be involved in using their spiritual gifts in the body of believers where they attend, but the team decides if they are far enough along in the process to take on a teaching opportunity or ongoing responsibilities that involve spiritual leadership. Let me remind you that only God gets to decide where and when his servants can be used, so this oversight is just for the time of formal restoration. We all know too many people who want to always remind people of their past failures and be the gatekeeper to stop God from ever using them again.

Finally, the team will decide when and if the person is ready to be declared fully restored and capable of returning to ministry. Again, it most probably will not be the same position they had when they fell, and it might not be returning to a similar position.

However, the goal is to remember that God uniquely crafted and gifted this person for the body of Christ, and nowhere in Scripture does it indicate that Jesus throws away and quits using the repentant broken brother. The ultimate goal of this process is for the team to arrive at the place where they believe the restoree is healthy enough spiritually and reconnected relationally to the point they can affirm the use of their gifts and callings.

To be certain, that person is forgiven by God and restored by God, but having a team that will put their good names on the line to stand with the one whose reputation has been marred is a gift to the fallen that cannot be overestimated. For that reason, the people on the team need to be unashamed of the work of restoration and unashamed of the person being restored.

Along the way, some of the usual responsibilities of being associated with a team will be required. Someone will have to take notes, documents will need to be crafted, meetings will need to be scheduled, and mediation will need to be experienced. Members of the team will need to have some gifts in these areas and a willingness to use those gifts.

Traffic Manager

I started my working career in radio in northwest Tennessee at a small FM station in a very small market. I was blessed to be able to work my way through school among several stations in that area. One of the more interesting job titles I once held at a small station was Traffic Manager.

Everyone who knew that thought I was the guy who gave the traffic reports on the radio. There were not at that time any four-lane roads in our county, so as you might imagine, the role had nothing to do with traffic. It was a position that directed the flow of information between the sales, production, and on-air departments. My job was to make sure the right hand knew what the left hand was doing, and to make sure the right hand was getting along with the left hand.

The further along you go in the team process of restoration, the more traffic managing you have to do. At the beginning, much of it is about the restoree and their immediate needs both spiritually and physically. Then, as you progress through the process, you find there are many stakeholders that need to have input. Some of those stakeholders are still angry and need someone to talk to them other than the person who offended them. At other times, team members will be sitting down with the restoree and the people who are hurt by his actions. They will also be asking people on behalf of the restoree to give him or her another chance to utilize his gifts, so there will need to be some written and personal interactions with people other than those on the team. In essence, the team will manage the flow of information between the former ministry, family, current church, and the restoree.

In that role, the team will be the arbiter of when and how apologies will be issued, when and if public acknowledgement of restoration will be done, and exactly what restoration means in the life of this particular person. They will be expected to put into writing a public letter regarding the restoree, whether that is to release him to pursue ministry, to acknowledge his efforts but recommend against future ministry, or to recommend further remediation.

Balance of Gifts

Every team needs different skills, gifts, talents, and abilities to be successful, and this one is no different. In addition to willingness and special relationships, it is important that the team be balanced in their spiritual gifts.

Every person on the team cannot be a strong leader and everyone cannot have the gift of mercy. It is also important to note that while the dominant gift of prophecy is not usually a good fit as a member of a restoration team, people with a mix of prophecy and mercy seem to be particularly useful to the process. That mix can be a little like searching for a unicorn, but it is good to not just discount people because they are high in prophetic gifts. Take a look further to see what gifts they have that balance that out.

A person who is high in mercy but has some prophecy or vice versa finds it much easier to hold the restoree accountable without crushing them in the process.

It is also helpful to find a balance of people that are respected across differing demographics. The larger the churches involved in the pain of the event, the less likely any one person will have influence across the broad spectrum. When a team is seeking to give validity to a person's restorative process, the people watching are more interested in the opinions of those on the team than the opinion of the one being restored.

It is important that they embody respect from different groups. Because of this, it is essential that they meet the Biblical admonition to be above reproach, though they may or may not be ordained. The reality is that they are putting their good name and reputation behind the restoree, whose name and reputation have been called into question, so theirs must be stellar.

One time in a sermon on using your gifts in the church, I quoted Rick Warren who said every tuba player needs a band, and that I had never seen a tuba soloist. I was inundated that week from church members with video clips of tuba solos, so I suppose I was wrong. However, I stand by my assertion that any person with a heart to restore hurting leaders and any hurting leader in need of restoration desperately needs a team. Restoration is a team sport.

Before You Move On

The restorative process requires a willingness on the part of the broken; a clearly defined process; and a group of people who have both the skills and willingness to take on a project. I am not good with my hands, though in recent years I have learned a lot on YouTube. I have always admired men who were patient enough to take an old rusted-out car or a run-down farmhouse and patiently restore it to its former glory. When you find those people in your church who can look at a broken man or woman and see them not for who they are but who they can be again, you have the makings of a restoration team.

For Further Thought:

1. What do you think you bring to the table as a restoration team member?

2. Who in your church and professional affiliations seems to have a bent toward restoration coupled with spiritual gifts, demeanor, and skills that would make them a good restoration team member?

3. Have you ever watched a person try to get back on their feet without the benefit of a team? What were your observations about how people reacted to them and were they successful long term?

Chapter 16

Restoration is a Covenant Driven Process

Each person that indicates a desire to be partnered with a team for spiritual restoration is given a covenant to review before entering into the process. Covenants are signed documents that reflect a deeply heartfelt desire by the restoree to come under the spiritual authority and direction of a team of leaders who are committed to the process and committed to the restoree. The basic covenant may be changed, shortened, or lengthened depending on the circumstances of the person in need of restoration, but most processes involve pretty much the same components.

In the next chapter is a blank covenant over which I claim no originality or authorship. It is just the original document that my team used and has been adapted over time as we saw needs for improvement and change. I have sought out the author of the covenant but have been unable to get anyone to claim originality of it.

Long Hollow Baptist Church in Hendersonville, Tennessee is as close as I can get. The Pastor Emeritus, Mike Dawson, who helped lead my own restoration team, tells me he got the basics from them and adapted it to my situation.

Covenant is a Biblical Concept

Many pastors and churches struggle with the idea of a written covenant since it has not been a staple in many denominations. However, in our church family, we talk a lot about covenant from the very beginning. Membership in our church is based on a signed covenant that clearly outlines the expectations of people who say God has led them to live in community together. These expectations, as you might imagine, are not rocket science, but simple commitments to living in unity, common support and ministry, Biblical treatment of one another, and so on. When I introduced the idea to a 140-year-old, traditional Baptist congregation, it was met with some skepticism and even questions that it seemed a bit too formal for what had long been an informal structure. Yet, in practice, it has proven to be a valuable tool in helping the membership maintain healthy relationships and guard the reputation of Jesus and His church in our community.

During the season when we were moving from traditional Baptist membership toward Covenant membership, we were often asked if covenant is a Biblical concept. If you are reading this book, you probably are deep enough in the Word of God that you don't need to be convinced; but the short answer is that it is, in fact, scriptural.

Consider Exodus 19:5, just before we get to the mother of all covenants, the ten commandments. "Now therefore, if you will indeed obey my voice and keep my covenant, you shall be my treasured possession among all peoples, for all the earth is mine."

Psalm 108:5-11 reminds us that God never forgets His covenant commitments. "He remembers his covenant forever, the word that he commanded, for a thousand generations, the covenant that he made with Abraham, his sworn promise to Isaac, which he confirmed to Jacob as a statute, to Israel as an everlasting covenant, saying, 'To you I will give the land of Canaan as your portion for an inheritance.'"

Jesus himself said in Matthew 26:28, "For this is My blood of the covenant, which is poured out for many for the forgiveness of sins." The author of Hebrews said in 9:15, "Therefore he is the mediator of a new covenant, so that those who are called may receive the promised eternal inheritance, since a death has occurred that redeems them from the transgressions committed under the first covenant."

The marriage ceremony I use points out that covenants and contracts are very different. A contract is a legally binding document, but most are written by attorneys and such that a good attorney can find a way to legally break it. Covenants are heart to heart between two parties. They are designed to keep each party in the process even when it gets uncomfortable. While they are both signed documents, covenants carry much more weight than contracts.

The Value of Covenant

Much of the value of the covenant for the restoree is what it communicates to everyone involved. In the initial conversations, I explain the value to the restoree of having clear expectations, steps to work on, and benchmarks. Beyond the restoree, though, a covenant has great value to both the team and the greater faith community that has been affected by the decisions of the restoree.

For the team, it provides clear boundaries and expectations. Often, the only goal of the restoree is to get a clean bill of health as fast as he or she can so they can go back to vocational ministry. That is why we have stressed in this book and clearly state in the covenant that the process carries with it no promise of an endorsement to return to vocational ministry.

As we have stated elsewhere, that is not the purview of the team anyway. God is ultimately the owner, Lord, and master of the restoree, and it is completely up to the owner what He does with His restored property. Not only is that not the decision of the restoration team, but it is also not the decision of the restoree. The covenant draws a clear picture of what the person can and cannot expect from the team.

There is another payoff to the covenant process that may not be readily visible to the restoree or the team for some time as the process unfolds. Having a covenant in place is comforting and encouraging to those whose lives have been affected by the choices made by the restoree. (We have said all along that restoration is not only for those who have made bad choices, but even those who have been injured often do things in response that wound themselves or others.)

The covenant is a tangible and structured proof that everyone involved is taking the process seriously. It assures those who have been collateral damage to the events surrounding this person that they have not been forgotten, and the person is truly being held accountable for his actions and encouraged to deal redemptively with both his pain and their pain.

It does not happen nearly as often as it once did, but after I (Pete) returned to vocational ministry, I would from time to time run into someone I knew or someone who had known of me. The conversation would often start out uncomfortably with them saying something like, "Aren't you that preacher that blew it down in Columbia?" I learned early on that the way to answer that as a person who has failed and been restored is to say humbly, "Yes, I am. Would you like to hear what God did to restore me and bring me to this place since then?"

Being able to tell them the hard work of most of 2009-2010 and how it was driven by a team and a covenant, while not always causing them to rejoice, at least lets them know I saw and treated those events seriously. It will be a valuable tool to the restoree long after the process is over as a "period at the end of the sentence."

In the eyes and minds of some people, it will never be over; but the active participation in and completion of a covenant process gives the restoree a sense that while this season will always be a part of God's great story in my life, it is just that - a season. The completion of a covenant process allows the restoree to move confidently into the next season of his life knowing he is not leaving behind unfinished business.

Covenant Is Rarely Fun

For the pastor and church who want to make restoration an ongoing ministry, or for the ones that just find themselves needing a road map at the time of upheaval, it should be noted that the covenant often acts as a deterrent to a person in need of restoration.

The covenant process brings into stark focus the reality of their motives. Often a broken servant will misunderstand the goals and purpose of restoration, or will harbor hidden (maybe even hidden to them) hopes for a quick and easy process and the covenant screams of hard work. Knowing there will be written assignments related to the events that led to their current condition, and an examination of the red lights they ran, or submitting to the oversight of a group of men, may be a bridge too far.

If the restoree is looking for a rubber stamp permission form to return to vocational ministry without doing the hard work of building structures over their fault lines to withstand the next earthquake, this process is not for them. Making them aware of the covenant process up front serves as a good barometer of how serious they are about getting right with God and others.

The covenant also has a way of causing us to slow down and do things right. Many of those who are wounded or broken find themselves in that position because they have lived a ministry life that is always pedal to the metal, full speed ahead. When life is moving that fast, one rarely has time to press into God and abide in Christ, much less let the Word dwell richly in us.

I struggled under the covenant with my team not only at the beginning but at various points along the journey. But the deliberate and exacting nature of the work and conversations taught me much about the pace of my life that had allowed me to get in that condition in the first place.

To continue an analogy, it is not hard to run a red light when you are already speeding. In fact, most of us have found ourselves realizing we were about to run a red light and making a split second decision to blow through it rather than throw on the brakes and risk losing control. Likewise, a covenant process allows you to pump the brakes rather than just rev the engine back to full speed.

More often than not, people who have suffered adverse events in their ministry will opt for a quick fix rather than engaging the process. Sometimes, the only reason they engage the covenant process is because they have no other alternative. If a ministry job presents itself, and they are unemployed, it makes sense in the natural to forego the long process and make sure you can pay the bills.

Many of the people who have come our way opt out quickly upon hearing the requirements of the covenant; and some decide as the conversations and prayer times unfold that they just are not willing to unpack some things in that environment.

That is not to say that everyone who declines or exits the covenant process is wrong about doing that. It is better to wait until you are strong enough and ready to tackle difficult things about yourself before entering the process. Others know something about their story that requires them to primarily seek professional or legal help before they have any conversation with a restoration team.

In fact, part of the initial conversation is that if they tell us something in the process that falls under "mandatory reporting" guidelines, that is what we will do. The covenant process up front weeds out those who are not serious and protects the team from getting in over their head. The last thing they want to do is try to force someone into submission who is really not interested in working through the process.

Covenant as Exit Ramp

Finally, the covenant serves as an exit ramp both for the restoree and the team, though neither should go into it looking for an exit. However, there are times when the process just does not work.

The restoree may feel like the team is being too slow, too harsh, or too one-sided in their dealings with him or her. On the other hand, when the work gets difficult the team may find the restoree either purposely or subconsciously will not or cannot do the hard work required. Other times, even after agreeing to the covenant, a restoree may act outside the covenant agreement without the permission or oversight of the team.

Whatever the case, a covenant clearly spells out expectations for both the team and the restoree, neither of whom should end the process lightly and without prayer. We are all broken people, and broken people do broken things. Grace should be exercised in the process even when things are not going well; but if you need an exit ramp, it is there.

Before You Move On

The big hairy unspoken word of covenant relationships is commitment. The leader has to be committed; the church has to be committed to the process if not the person; and the broken servant needs to be committed. Having a covenant process in place makes it easier to gauge the commitment of all the parties involved.

For Further Thought:

1. Does your belief structure allow you to embrace a covenant agreement process? What about your church or other spiritual leadership? Why or why not?

2. What would you say to a fellow minister who is in need of restorative ministry but pushes back against the idea of a covenant process?

3. Can you think of other reasons a covenant process might be valuable for someone who is either far from God or has been far from God and is trying to find his way back?

Chapter 17

A Model Covenant

What follows is a template of a covenant that your leadership team can adapt and adjust to the circumstances of those who come to you for restoration. Remember, I claim no originality for this document, and what you see in front of you has evolved and changed over the years that we have been using it. The one I am giving you here is very close to the original covenant that my personal restoration team used with me in 2009. I have made some tweaks to it as we have gone along and found that some things worked better than others.

Remember that every time you use it, it needs to be tweaked further for the specific needs of the restoree at hand. However, be sure you do not tweak it so much that it begins to get watered down and is ineffective for the work it is supposed to do. The process will lead to a positive outcome if it is bathed in prayer, and each team member and restoree fulfills their role in the covenant.

RESTORATION COVENANT BETWEEN RESTORATION TEAM OF (CHURCH) AND (RESTOREE)

This Covenant between the Restoration Team of CHURCH NAME (referred hereinafter as restoration team) and RESTOREE NAME (referred to hereinafter as the candidate) is for the purpose of agreeing to enter the process of restoration as stated in the following sections of this document and continuing in the process to a satisfactory completion determined by the restoration team and Church Leadership.

This covenant is entered effective (DATE.) This covenant shall continue until the process is completed as defined in the covenant. If at any time during this process the candidate does not follow the requirements of this covenant, then the covenant will be deemed to be "broken" and will end. Any amendments to this plan must be approved by the restoration team. If during this process the restoration team and the candidate agree that full restoration under the terms of this covenant cannot be reached, it will terminate.

The Purpose of Restoration

The purpose of this process of restoration is to aid the candidate's own personal and spiritual healing and the healing of his important relationships. This process of restoration has no time limits and no guarantees, even though the completion of the restoration process may include the return to vocational ministry.

The Steps of Restoration

1. The restoration process will be under-girded by prayer, supported by Scripture, particularly the sixth chapter of Galatians, and led by the Holy Spirit.

2. This Restoration Covenant with the approval of the (LEADERSHIP TEAM) of (CHURCH) will be reported to the church by letter and will be accompanied by a letter from the candidate in which he acknowledges that he has submitted to this covenant, he apologizes for the pain and confusion his actions have brought to the church and the community, and states that this process is not an effort to return to the leadership role in which he failed. A similar letter will be sent by the restoration team and the candidate to the local organizations to which he answered or with which he served.

3.   The candidate will actively engage in another church and come under its care and discipline. That church will agree to accept the candidate under these conditions and will be approved by the restoration team.

4.   The candidate will complete the appropriate steps in the process before returning to any speaking situations or other public ministry. This means the candidate is encouraged to actively investigate secular employment.

5.   The candidate will satisfactorily complete professional counseling for him and his family to deal with the issues acknowledged from this event.

6.   Restoration team will determine the following:
     a)   Frequency, date, and time of meetings.
     b)   Place meetings will be conducted
     c)   Meeting agendas

7.   A member of the restoration team shall be appointed to journal the content of the meetings as well as assignments and action plans and other important records.

8.   Candidate will keep a journal of his progress, carefully recording assignments, topics discussed, positive and negative reactions during the meeting, things that helped and things that hurt, and other entries important to the restoration and his journey through the process.

9.   Candidate will write out a full and complete confession. He must:
     a)   Come clean with no excuses or defenses.
     b)   Include details of the events that occurred but not necessarily too graphic.
     c)   Include dates, places, events, and again, emphasis on coming clean. Hide nothing, including how you got caught and/or what made you decide to confess.

10. With the assistance of the restoration team, an accountability group will be established.

11. A repair strategy will be determined and shall include but not be limited to:
   a) Sensitivity to "godly sorrow" (conviction) of candidate.
   b) Fruit (acts) of repentance
   c) Confession, (agreeing with God) (Where's the candidate's heart?)
   d) Facing the offended and properly seeking forgiveness.
   e) A life-habit strategy developed to guard against a future failure.

12. The candidate will write out a list of contributing patterns and practices that led or contributed to his failure and sin.

13. Restoration team and the candidate will construct a plan to correct contributing factors. This includes compiling a list of "Red Lights Ran." No one can have a moral crash without running a series of moral red lights first. The candidate will:
   a) Make a careful list of how he ignored moral red lights on the way to his crash.
   b) Develop a list of moral red lights (with the aid of the restoration team) that he will NOT run ever again.

14. At a time and place arranged by the restoration team, the candidate will meet with another minister/lay leader who went through a failure and was subsequently excluded from ministry/service but later fully restored by the Lord through the restoration process. (Note: the candidate may be called upon and should be willing to do this for others once restored.)

15. A careful review of the above restoration steps and the degree of completion for each of the steps will be conducted together with the (CHURCH LEADERSHIP), and restoration team. Other recommendations and steps may be forthcoming and required as a result of this meeting.

16. Any pending steps will then be addressed and resolved to the satisfaction of the recommending leadership groups.

17. Having successfully worked through all previous requirements, the candidate will be asked to meet with the (CHURCH LEADERSHIP) and restoration team to verbally share his testimony and journey of restoration.

18. The candidate will then prepare a written and signed version of his restoration testimony to be reviewed, updated (if required) and placed in both the candidate's journal and be recorded by the restoration team which will then be properly filed with the church.

19. Upon the unanimous agreement of the (CHURCH LEADERSHIP) and the restoration team, the candidate will be declared "fully restored" and a letter of this declaration will be issued on church stationery and presented to the candidate and a copy will also be placed in the candidate's journal.

This RESTORATION COVENANT is entered into by:

Restoree

_____

Team Member
#1_____

Team Member
#2_____

Team Member
#3_____

Date_____

Before You Move On

Having read the model covenant, you may be overwhelmed by the scope and depth of it. It takes very little time to bulldoze an historic building and start the process of rebuilding a brand new facility where it once stood. However, if you want to take the time to restore the old building to its former glory, there is much more work to be done. This covenant is not a bulldozer but a tool in the hands of a master craftsman (God) repairing a valuable item. It takes time.

For Further Thought:

1. What is your initial reaction to the restoration covenant? Is it too much? Too legalistic? Too harsh? Why?

2. If you are reading this book, it is probably because you know someone who needs your help. How do you think they will react to this covenant?

3. If your church were going to officially engage in a restoration ministry either one time or ongoing, what group or groups of leaders would need to be kept in the loop?

Chapter 18

Is That Necessary?

Even for the person who understands their need for covenant restoration and is willing to do the hard work, there will be pieces of the covenant that make them uncomfortable or that they want to skip over, perhaps feeling they do not need that and it is a waste of time. Chester Vaughn, a church education specialist of many years past was in the twilight of his career when I was just beginning. Over dinner after spending a day of consulting with me about my church and our shortcomings, he said this: "The best laid plans of mice and men...eventually devolve into work." The value of each piece of the covenant is that we don't know what we don't know and the work reveals what we need and what we don't need.

Along the way, you will find some of the processes to seemingly overlap and become redundant. While each step of the process has its own particular meaning and purpose, it is true that some of it begins to feel redundant, especially looking at it initially and then later in the process. There are many places where redundancy is boring and unnecessary, but in processes of life and death-like medical procedures, airplane inspections, and industrial safety, built-in redundancies are the norm. We all agree that those redundancies are important and want them to keep doing those things to keep us safe. Helping a fallen or broken believer return to significant relationships in their lives and find a way back to productive service in the Kingdom of God can be no less important.

The value of redundancy is that we may not have known something about ourselves or maybe were even too ashamed to talk about something during one step, but we are aware and ready to deal with it later in the process. I doubt the framers of my original covenant were aware of that reality when they walked with me in this journey. If you are doing a one-time restoration project, you may never experience that; but the experience of nearly ten years of restoring broken members and broken ministers has convinced me not to skip a step in the process.

The rest of this chapter focuses on some of the components of covenant restoration and a brief reasoning behind each. We will assume that some of them are so straightforward as to need no defense.

Church Participation

Where a restoree can attend church can be discussed, but whether or not they attend church cannot. Almost every person that comes to us wanting to get better or get help is out of church and most of them at some time have been a pastor or staff member. Why would someone who spent their life in the church not be regularly attending church and using what gifts they have at whatever level is available to them?

Sometimes a lack of church attendance belies a condition of the heart, revealing that they were active in church because they were paid to be so, not because they were actively living in community as described in the Bible. In fact, it is very easy for a minister to feel all alone even though they are always in church.

Another reason for failure to attend church is a general sense of worthlessness if he has been fired by a church, committed sin that has become public, or disappointed people. A more subtle reason is that most ministers don't know how to select a church, having just moved from one vocational assignment to the next. The sad reality is that many churches don't know what to do with a broken servant, so they feel cold and distant when he tries to attend. That is

211

why the restoration team has to give leadership to that process.

Another aspect of the covenant says that the "candidate will complete the appropriate steps in the process before returning to any speaking situations or other public ministry." That means when he does attend another church and begin to plug in, he may not feel he has anything to offer. However, I (Pete) began attending a large church a few miles up the road almost immediately and while my team did not allow me to take on any speaking engagements or teaching assignments, they urged me to find a way and a place to serve. When I found my way back to God, I rediscovered my love for prayer and served by leading a prayer time each Sunday during one of the three services, praying for the pastor, the work of the Spirit, and any specific requests that came from the previous services.

One of the most valuable insights I received in that year at The People's Church in Franklin, Tennessee, was the importance of life in a community group. Most pastors either fail to take time or simply do not have time to get connected to a Sunday School Class or Small Group. That is sometimes driven by fear of showing favoritism and our concern that people will think we don't care as much about them as we do those we are doing life with.

My year with that Tuesday night community group fed my soul, gave me new friendships, and taught me the value of making a habit of staying connected that I have continued now through ten years of return to ministry. I believe now that if I had the kind of relationships in my previous church that I have here, I may not have gone as far as I did. It was not the fault of that church, but it was my own lack of understanding. It is a very good thing for a broken church leader to learn how to be a servant and participant. (As an aside, it also gave me a lot more sympathy for those who work in the real world and can't make it to my meetings.)

Confession

The covenant says "Candidate will write out a full and complete confession. He must: Come clean with no excuses or defenses; include details of the events that occurred, but not necessarily too graphic; and include dates, places, and events and again, there is an emphasis on coming clean. Hide nothing, including how you got caught and/or what made you decide to confess."

People on teams and several candidates have pushed back on the idea of the written confession, even asking if the team and process is not setting itself up to be God by asking for it. However, this confession is not the same as a Biblical confession that agrees with God about your sin and the resulting discipline. It is a clear acknowledgement of how far one's sin or brokenness has taken them. There is nothing more painful in the process than this written confession, but it is crucial to the healing process. Even now, many years later for me (Pete), it is hard for me to verbalize the journey I was on when the wheels ran off. Like all humans, even when I am trying to be stone cold honest, I want to downplay parts of the story and ignore others. It is prideful human nature to want to look the best we can, even when we have been exposed.

One of the unforeseen values of a written confession is when rumors start flying around. Unfortunately, the church is a ripe grapevine at times and rumors can run rampant. When someone says to the restoration team, "You have no idea what he or she did," based on a rumor or a perception they have, the team can say, "Yes, we do!" A broken and hurting minister has no standing to defend himself, but a restoration team can do so when they know everything and know the person is doing all they can to be right with God and restored to their family and friends.

The confession makes the process complete. By not writing the confession, the restoree can hide some of the more sordid parts of the story, even from himself. The further one is removed from the events that led to their crash, the more those events can be hidden and pushed beneath the surface. However, if they are not confessed, repented of, and dealt with, it is almost certain they will burst out again somewhere down the line. We are only as sick as our secrets, and we all need a safe place to expose our secrets. By the way, if the team is not a safe place to do that, you have the wrong team.

A List of "Red Lights Ran"

We have alluded in a few places in this book to the "red lights" analogy from this covenant. Specifically, the document says "Restoration team and the candidate will construct a plan to correct contributing factors. This includes compiling a list of 'Red Lights Ran.' No one can have a moral crash without running a series of moral red lights first. The candidate will: Make a careful list of how he ignored moral red lights on the way to his crash and develop a list of moral red lights (with the aid of the restoration team) that he will NOT run ever again."

For all those who drive, this is an easy analogy to wrap our heads around. As I write this, I have taken a week away from the church to go to the beach and finish the manuscript. (Somebody has to do it!) On the way down here, I was waiting on a light to turn when I looked and saw that no one was coming and had a momentary lapse of sanity. Thinking it was a four way, I made my left turn. Thankfully no police or cars were coming and I lived to tell about it. It was an accident but many times, we see a yellow and speed up but not quite enough. That is not an accident.

For the restoree looking back, he will notice two kinds of red lights he ran. These are not overt sins he committed, but instead are roadblocks God puts in his way when he is about to commit a presumptive sin or experience the big earthquake. I have written previously about my wife's plea for me to see a doctor, which I ignored, and how on the night of my earthquake a dear friend texted me and I did not read the signs. There were other red lights where I refused to stop and ultimately, God had to deal with me. Writing out the list of red lights, and there are many, has helped me to construct a plan that has made this last ten years of ministry so much more fulfilling and rewarding.

Facing the Music

Much of the crisis in the life of a broken servant is the burden of carrying his secrets alone. That is true both before a public earthquake and afterward. Before, there is the burden of keeping his secrets whether they are sins or habits or just deep emotional wounds. After the earthquake, there is the burden of reputation repair and control. We spend an enormous amount of time developing a reputation and then find ourselves tyrannized by it. The value of several of the meetings covered in the covenant is that they force the person out of their shell and give them experience in telling the story and weaving it into the fabric of what God has done and is continuing to do in them.

The restoree is asked to meet with another minister who himself has been through a restorative process and exchange stories. The value of doing that early in the process is because the restoree needs to feel some hope that not only is this process productive, and that he will survive it, he also sees someone who God is using post-earthquake to minister to him. In this component, he gains some hope that this ugly part of his story can be used by God, and that he will indeed see God exchange beauty for the ashes of his life.

At some point in the process, he meets with the leadership of the church overseeing his restoration to give his restoration testimony. It is not another apology or confession, but a simple acknowledgement that this thing has happened and here is the story of what God has been doing with me and in me since then. To be clear, it is not a re-confession of the event, but is a quick acknowledgement of the event followed by the story of how God has worked since then. It is a further step in the integration of this season into his life story.

Along the way, depending on the specific details of the candidate's journey, there may be meetings with family members, former church staff and leadership, and even ministry colleagues. Often, the person is so remorseful and even shamed by their failure that without some coaching and help, they will never reach out to those groups. At the same time, those groups and individuals may not know how to reach out, or even if that person wants to talk to them. Having the restoration team set up meetings and act as a wingman is a great help.

The Accountability Team

A person is never more vulnerable to sinking into deep depression, sin, or addiction than they are when they have failed publicly and feel they have no hope of ever putting things back together again. It is precisely at that moment of greatest vulnerability that they need an accountability team more than ever. So, why does the Restoration Team not fill that role?

The Restoration Team is selected mostly by someone else; is essentially working in a role of spiritual authority over the person; and has a vested interest in making sure that person does not fail again; so it might be too harsh if they come forward with a current temptation or failure. The accountability team is selected entirely by the restoree with the knowledge of the restoration team. They can offer reservations or encouragement, but in the end, the accountability team belongs to the person needing restoration. In a couple of cases, there has been some conversation between the accountability team and the restoration team; most often, the only role for the restoration team in accountability is to make sure the restoree has a team of people with whom he can be honest. You may find the restoree has already moved to develop that accountability team.

This team's purpose is weekly interaction with the restoree for encouragement, comfort, and spiritual growth. The restoration team is a monthly meeting and has as much responsibility to the church as they do the restoree. The accountability group is a band of brothers and their focus is the spiritual health and protection of the restoree. One of the unfortunate byproducts of this is that there will be times when the teams are not in agreement on next steps, but both fulfill a role that is needed. You will find the accountability team is most often ready to release the candidate back into ministry service before the restoration team. Again, this is caused by the fact they are engaged solely with the restoree while the other team is engaging church, family, candidate, and others.

You also have the reality that the hidden faults in the life of a fallen brother do not just go away when there is an earthquake. He still has the same hurts, habits, and hang-ups that he did before. Yet, he knows the restoration team is giving oversight and has the authority to say he is ready to return to vocational service or volunteer service in the church. He or she is going to be very reluctant to talk to the restoration team about the temptations he is facing. The accountability team gives a safe place to be honest about such things.

Counseling

I have a love-hate relationship with professional counseling that I won't go into at length here, but let it suffice to say I have seen people greatly aided in their recovery by a good counselor, and I have seen people wallow for years in unproductive counseling. However, like going to one bad restaurant will not make me quit eating out, one bad counseling outcome does not overshadow the value of talented individuals who God has uniquely gifted to guide hurting people through processes of healing.

Every restoration need is different, but often marriage counseling is needed or the effects on the children are such that they need help processing what has happened. I almost always insist that the restoree has at least a little interaction with a professional counselor who is also a believer. That is again, because the thing that felled them is not usually the core issue or hidden fault. Counselors know the right questions to ask and the right plans to correct those things. Additionally, there are often things they need to discuss that no one on the restoration team is qualified or prepared to discuss.

Much of this book has been about building a culture of restoration in your church, and one way to do that is to be prepared to help broken people get the counseling they need. Most often, a restoree has lost a job or has increased expenses due to the event that brought them to you and finds it hard to pay for counseling. Your church can stand in the gap for them by having a list of partner organizations that offer free or reduced fee counseling for your people. Some churches keep a line item available in their budget to be used at the discretion of the pastor to fund counseling needs throughout the year. The pastor or another staff member has complete discretion and when a member or restoree gets financial aid for counseling, that pastor or staff member is the only one that knows. Often, the need for in-depth restoration and counseling can be avoided if the church is open about helping people get help for the issues in their lives before the earthquake happens. An ounce of prevention is worth a pound of cure.

Restorative Culture Churches see the need for spouses and children of the restoree to seek counseling as well and are willing to help underwrite some of the cost. We encourage the person to pay some of the cost as people tend to value what they invest in. Even if the person is unemployed, we find some ways for them to give some sweat equity to the church or a partner organization in order to not feel like a charity case.

Before You Move On

From the very beginning of this book, the point has been made that events give birth to processes. It is one thing to repent and seek forgiveness, but another thing altogether to enter into a process whereby wounds can be healed and health can be restored. Each of these components of the process are important and contribute to the overall success of the process. To skip one because you do not understand the need or because it is uncomfortable would be a mistake.

For Further Thought:

1. Are you comfortable with the idea of a written confession as outlined in the covenant? Why or why not?

2. What advice would you give to someone developing an accountability team? How has the accountability process worked for you?

3. Does your faith family value counseling as a tool for recovery? What can you do in your church's current structure to help families avoid the earthquake before it happens?

Chapter 19

The Period at the End of the Sentence

We always begin the conversation with a person seeking restoration with the reality that the process has no prescribed length and that it can be as much as twelve to eighteen months. We do not measure progress by the calendar but by the mental, physical, and most importantly, the spiritual health of both the restoree and the significant relationships of his life. This is not an easy thing to read, and it is even harder to put into writing; but at the risk of sounding trite, you will know when it is time. For our processes with various candidates over the years, we have been in the process for as few as ten months and for as long as two years.

Of course, most contacts you have with fallen and broken leaders will never get this far. Most count the cost of the process to be too great and never get involved, while others say they want it, but sadly are not yet ready to get real about the fault lines in their lives, nor do the hard work required on their part.

Yet, for that one out of three, in our experience, that actually makes it through and the team feels they are ready to be released again into whatever ministry the Father has planned for them, there needs to be a clear finish line, just as the covenant signing was the clear starting line. This chapter will deal with some ways to bring a healthy process to an end.

The Power of Celebration

Far better writers have written about the Prodigal Son story from Luke 15, so I won't try to retell the story here, but I do want to remind you of one component. When the Father saw the son coming, he ran to him, embraced him, and then set about the business of planning a party. "But the father said to his servants, 'Bring quickly the best robe, and put it on him, and put a ring on his hand, and shoes on his feet. And bring the fattened calf and kill it, and let us eat and celebrate. For this my son was dead, and is alive again; he was lost, and is found.' And they began to celebrate."

Much of the church has forgotten the concept of party and celebration. I recall many years ago hearing Tony Campolo tell the story of visiting an African-American church for the first time and accidentally wandering into a funeral. As Tony could do, he told the story with great fanfare and it ended with the choir singing boisterously "When the Saints Go Marching In" as the pallbearers danced down the aisle carrying the deceased on their shoulders. His summary statement was that this particular church turned a funeral into a party where most of the evangelical movement has turned what God intended to be a party into a funeral.

There is great value in ceremony and celebration and the process of restoration is no different. Our Jewish friends have for centuries, rooted in their Old Testament faith, valued greatly the celebrations that mark the end of one season and the beginning of the next. Restoration is a season in that person's life. I am never defensive when someone asks about that season in my life, but I do know it was just a season and I speak that to them.

One of the ways that season came to an end for me was a reception organized by the restoration team and hosted by the church where I was pastor when I crashed. It had been over a year since the process started and I was living in the same town, but I had not seen most of the people in the church. Part of that was at the request of the team so as not to confuse the membership that I might be coming back. Honestly, the greater reason was my fear early on of what they would say or think or that it might be awkward. Shortly after the reception, I had the opportunity to return to a short term ministry assignment to get my feet wet and when I finished that, the door to serve where I currently pastor opened up. Had that reception not happened, I probably would have left town without ever seeing most of those people again.

The event included a worship time where their current pastor spoke on restoration and its value, followed by a time to meet and greet in the fellowship hall. For me, it was literally the first time I had been in the building other than through a side door to meet with the team in over a year. Closure is a word that is used too loosely in grief settings of all kinds, but it provided kind of a closure for me that made living there and later returning to visit easier. For those church members who loved me and were either disappointed or confused, it gave the ones that wanted it the ability to say, "This thing happened and we are going to be okay, and Pastor Pete is going to be okay."

We have used different models to conduct that final celebration over the years in different circumstances. A church lay leader may not have affected the entire church and the celebration needs to be with those he affected. A pastor may have wounded a church past the point of them being involved so the celebration has to be somewhere or something else. Each situation is different.

In one particular situation, the young pastor had an emotional affair with a woman in the church, but the church was already very unhealthy. He came clean with his wife and his deacons, who promptly fired him. In the process of the restoration season, we had led him to write a letter of apology and ask permission to stand before the church at an appointed time to read it to the people. When they declined that, we asked if the deacons would read it to the church, which they also declined. Only God knows if that was right or wrong, so this is no way a judgment of their motives or hearts. However, it made it very clear they would not be open to a restoration celebration of any kind.

In that case, we hosted a celebration at the church of one of the team members near the home area of the young pastor and invited anyone who had been part of his ministry in the past to participate. Each of the participating churches were represented there that day and the tone of the service was one of joy that this one who would have been shipwrecked from then on, was now restored and ready should God choose to use him again in a leadership role.

Sadly, we do not get to do as many of the celebrations as we would like. I am convinced, however, that a process that ends well deserves to be celebrated. The celebration is not saying that person is now returning to ministry. Remember, God is the ultimate decider and our only job is to restore according to Galatians 6:1. What He decides to do at that point is up to Him, but even if the restored servant is never again called on to serve as a church leader, the process and the end of this season is worth celebrating.

The Final Report

In addition to the celebration, the team needs to provide a final report to any of the stakeholders that have been actively involved in the process. Perhaps, this is the step that is hardest on some of you as members of the team. Up to this point, you may not necessarily agree with everything, but you are almost coming across as a hero because you have stepped into the gap when a fellow Christ follower was at their lowest and most vulnerable. Now, you are being called on to publicly and forever declare that you believe this person is restored. Each report will be different, but a team member may struggle to put his name on the line for someone who has fallen, especially if it is a fall that we find personally distasteful. A team member needs to know going in, they will need to do this. If they don't believe that under any circumstances they could see God using this person again, then they do not need to be part of the team.

REPORT OF RESTORATION TEAM
COMPLETION OF RESTORATION COVENANT WITH
Rev. John E. (Pete) Tackett

Scripture clearly teaches us that no man should judge another (Mt. 7:1) but at the same time, it teaches us that man has the duty to restore someone who has been overtaken in a fault (Galatians 6:1ff). Conversely, forgiveness and restoration ultimately are something only our Heavenly Father can accomplish (1 Peter 5:10). With this in mind and with humility, we the undersigned members of the Restoration Team submit this report on the completion of the process of restoration of Rev. John E. (Pete) Tackett.

Beginning with our first meeting October 27, 2009, Bro. Pete was submissive and committed to seeing this process through. Although the agreement had several points of action that we felt would benefit him physically, mentally, and spiritually, the overall process was deemed more important than the completion of a sequence of tasks.

Bro. Pete graciously and with humility completed each task we asked him to do. We received reports from his physician and counselor that he is capable of resuming ministerial duties and we confirmed via various other means that he had completed the other tasks as well. More importantly, it became very apparent to us personally that the Pete we interact with today, is vastly different than the Pete we observed during our first meeting.

It is our sentiment that although Bro. Pete made some very unwise choices during a dark time in his life and as a result violated some biblical principles such as being above reproach and losing trust of the people, we do not believe that Bro. Pete committed any sin that would disqualify him from serving in the ministry permanently.

With this in mind and knowing that only God has the ability to judge and restore, we can without hesitation state that as best we know how to facilitate these divine actions, we are glad to confirm that Bro. Pete has been restored by our Heavenly Father and is ready to resume ministerial duties as the Lord leads.

Note that I have eliminated the identifying information of the church and the four members of my team, but the body of writing in the image is exactly as it was presented to me. Through the years, I have worked with teams to tailor this to the unique needs and circumstances of the individual.

The final report should be clear, concise, and short. It is not everyone's business what all happened in the process. The one issued to me was one page and covers the key things. (See image.) It needs to be forward-looking and not go into detail about the past. Too often, people in ministry talk too much. By this point in the process, the talking has been done and the primary purpose of this final report is to inform the leadership of the church overseeing the restoration and any others the team deems necessary of the completion of the process and the team's expressed opinion that the restoree has now been restored to usefulness in whatever position God chooses to place them in the Kingdom. If there is an understanding that the person has done all they can to be fully restored and are right with God, but the team is concerned about their family or mental health or some other reason that might hinder their return to a ministry position, it can be expressed here. However, the main reason for issuing a final report is the successful completion of the process. If the overseeing church or anyone else needs to be informed of the early termination or failure of the process, it can be done in person or in a paragraph long document. Again, the reason for the failure is not important for everyone to know, just that restoration was not attainable in this case, at this time. The actual timing and writing of the report should be a team exercise and serves as a clear finish line to the process.

The PostScript

Once the scheduled meetings are over, the processes have ended, and the hard work has been done, the restoration team, the church leadership team, colleagues, and former ministry partners still have a role to fill, especially if the recommendation of the team is that the person is now fit and prepared to return to a leadership position, either vocationally or as a volunteer. Just as he did in the beginning of the process, the restoree is going to need some traveling partners in the next phase of the journey.

Unfortunately, as we discussed early in this book, there are some people who, once you fail, write you off forever, but that is not everyone. However, human nature is what it is, and a person with a black mark on their service record is going to find it hard to be trusted by people again; especially those making decisions about who should be called to lead a ministry or church. It only makes sense that if you have two or more qualified candidates, you will be drawn to the one with the spotless record. It is the same principle that makes it so hard for a convicted felon to get a job. The team, the church, and the leaders cannot guarantee that will not happen to the restoree, but there are some ways they can pave the way for a smoother re-entry.

Letters of Recommendation

Team members can provide letters of recommendation that acknowledge the process but center on the skills and calling of the person. They can also help by reaching out to others who have been people of peace early in the process and who value the ministry of the restoree to also write letters of recommendation. I am going to excerpt a couple of those that were provided to me as examples.

"When I think about men in my life who have displayed transformation in the hands of God, Pete Tackett is one that I consider. I have known Pete for 12 years and have worked with him in Baptist associational life and summer camp ministry. Pete has invested himself in personal friendship and mentoring as well. In all of this, I have seen Pete sanctified in the Lord."

"Recently I have walked with Pete in some of his most difficult trials, and I have observed a man with a deep level of humility and transparency that only comes from a willingness to submit to the counsel of God and godly men for the glory of Jesus. Pete is now serving the Lord and others in a new capacity that is building Christ's Kingdom in a multitude of ways."

"I personally know that the time I spend with Pete Tackett enriches me in the Lord. When I think about Pete, he reminds me of the prophet Nathan, a man who spoke the word of God to David. Being in leadership, like David, I cherish Pete's counsel, wisdom, and understanding of grace, mercy, and godliness as he invests in my life. It is with utmost

confidence that I encourage you to seek a relationship with Pete, for you will be blessed in doing so."[25]
— *Matt Warren, Teaching Pastor, Coopertown Community Church, Coopertown, Tenn.*

"Regardless of where he preaches, Pete remains my pastor, my mentor, and my friend. His ministry to me and his impact in my life extend so much further than just the words that God has inspired him to offer from the pulpit. Pete's humble, transparent spirit continues to encourage and set an example for those who know him as he navigates both the mountains and the valleys of his walk. I am continually emboldened and refreshed by his zeal for the truth of Scripture and his willingness to set aside the traditions of men for the reality of Jesus Christ."[26]
— *Jason Whatley, attorney, friend, and former church member, Columbia, Tenn.*

Each of these men and several others provided me with letters that I could include with my resume when I spoke with a team seeking a pastor or staff member. One friend coached me in writing a resume that acknowledged my valley but looked ahead. You will notice that each one acknowledged the event but looked both at my past ministry efforts and what God could do with me in this new phase of life. It will be helpful if the restoration team coaches the restoree and helps him reach out to the right people who can and will write those recommendations. The "right people" selected do not need to look like a coverup, but should include those who knew him before and after the failure.

---

[25] Used with permission.
[26] Used with permission.

A Good Word

This one does not take much to explain. The word "benediction" is rooted in the Latin and means essentially "a good word." Once the team is finished with the process, team members and all those involved need to be in the business of helping that person get back on his feet by sharing a good word. When someone criticizes the now restored soldier, team members should be quick to change the direction of the conversation. They do not need to say it was not so bad or that the person has no right to feel that way, but they do need to point out the incredibly good work that person has put in to get back on his or her feet.

Furthermore, the team and church leaders should look for a way to help them get back to ministry in whatever role God has for them. One way that happens is keeping your eyes and ears open for a role for which you think the restoree is a good match and then make the appropriate recommendations. The restoration team should be available to serve as references to be listed on a resume if the restoree desires and should be useful in helping to distribute that resume.

Finally, just because you are restored and the team is dissolved doesn't mean the battle is over. Broken relationships may be restored to a new and healthy model, but many of them will never be the same again. Finding a role in ministry will be hard for some, and impossible for others. Former church members who seemed like lifelong friends may never return to the friendship. This is an unfortunate reality for those who have fallen off a high pedestal. The restoree is going to need some people that just pray for them and say an encouraging word when the going gets tough. They will need some people to fill the roles of those former friendships and relationships. They will need someone to buy them a cup of coffee and say a good word.

Epilogue

My friend, Pastor Don Pierson, once opined that because of some choices he made, he and his family were living in God's second best. He said the Bible is full of stories where God's perfect plan was thwarted either by the disobedience of a person or nation, or by the failure of someone to follow through.

Think about it. Adam and Eve were still blessed by God after being evicted from the Garden after the fall. David was still considered a man after God's own heart and was said to have "served the purpose of God in his own generation, fell asleep and was laid with his fathers and saw corruption" (Acts 13:36). His family was a mess and His people were caught in the vortex of his sin, but in the end, he lived in God's second best. Israel was so close to putting their feet in the promised land and then had to wander 40 years in the wilderness because of their idol worship. They ultimately got to enter the promised land, although the disobedient died in the wilderness. Moses had years of good ministry and led the people well right up to the point of death, even though he would only see and not enter the promised land. All and many more in the Bible lived in God's second best because of their personal failures.

Here is the thing, though: God's second best is not bad. For all those listed above, God continued to use them and they fulfilled God's purpose in one way or another. I (Pete) look back at the last 10 years and realize that I, too, have been living in the blessing of God's second best.

I would never presume to say that what happened to me, what I did, and how it ended, were caused by God. I believe in the sovereignty of God; but as I have noted in several places, there were red lights God put in front of me that would have stopped the series of events from unfolding over those several months. I ignored or ran those red lights. Just like what happens when you run a red light in your car, sometimes nothing happens and sometimes you wind up in a life-altering collision. Just because I ran the red lights and had the collision did not mean that God was either surprised by it or planned it. As my friend often says, "It just is what it is."

The truth is that I would never have looked from where I was as pastor of a large church with the salary, staff, resources, and respect that comes along with it and chosen to leave to embrace the ministry God has given me now. Yet, the longer I pastor this church and find a way to encourage pastors and other leaders who are struggling, the more thankful I am that God's second best is not too bad.

If I could go back and undo the damage and change the outcome for the people I let down, I would; but I do not yearn for that church, that ministry, that salary, or that respect. I still wince when I think of the shame, the pain, and the fallout, but I do not live my life thinking "What if...?" King David said in Psalm 16:6, "The lines have fallen for me in pleasant places; indeed, I have a beautiful inheritance." Having been lovingly restored by a merciful God at the hands of some Godly men, I can say with David, the lines for ME have fallen in pleasant places and I have a beautiful inheritance.

Although I would have never chosen this path, it is a privilege to share this journey with others who find themselves in the same place. In the words of Charles Stanley,[27] "Only those who have been through the fire are qualified to be firemen." It is a qualification I would not willingly pursue, but I refuse to waste it.

---

[27] Heard by the author - Dr. Charles Stanley, Pastor, First Baptist Church, Atlanta, GA, in a sermon delivered in Boone, NC, in April 1986.

Even as I was writing these last words, the phone rang and a bruised and beaten church planter was on the phone as a result of someone who had heard my story and thought I might be able to help him. He did not commit a "great transgression" but still needs a friend that understands when ministry goes sideways, and he needs a pathway both for him and his family back to spiritual health, and hopefully back to useful Kingdom service. I am energized by the opportunity to help him.

If, as you read this book, God stirs your spirit to want to help wounded soldiers, I promise you God will open your eyes to opportunity and they will find you. Carry on!

ABOUT THE AUTHORS

J. Pete Tackett

J. Pete Tackett is the Lead Pastor of Antioch Baptist
Church in Johnson City, Tennessee, and leads a loosely
organized network (with no name) whose primary goal is to
lead broken churches and broken servants to a place where
God can restore and redeploy them into useful service in His
Kingdom. Antioch Baptist Church, themselves a broken
church that God has restored and redeployed in the last
decade, serves as a willing home base and partner to this
network. Several current and former staff members have
taken their first steps back toward vocational ministry
through this partnership.

Pete began his education at Bethel College in McKenzie,
Tennessee until he ran out of money and transferred to East
Tennessee State where he studied communication and met
his wife. He then finished a Diploma from the Holston
Baptist Bible Institute, an outpost of what was then called
seminary extension by the Baptist Sunday School Board.

His ministry resume includes stints as youth pastor,
denominational consultant, co-pastor, and lead pastor. In
2016, he authored *re.Vital.ize: Lessons Learned in a Recovering
Church*. He has served on the advisory board for Youth
Evangelism Explosion International and as president of the
local chapter of Family Promise, a ministry to homeless
families with children. Currently, he is a Pastor-Connector for
Northeast Tennessee for the Tennessee Baptist Mission
Board and a team member of the Holston Baptist
Association's Church Replant and Revitalization Team.

Pete has been married to the former Lori Volkmann
since 1984 and together they have two adult children. Sarah is

233

31 and has served for extended periods of time in India and Indonesia as well as short term trips to Belize and several locations within the United States. Jonathan is married to Kelly and has served as a volunteer in student ministry, on a church plant survey team in Alaska, and has been on short term mission trips to Romania and several locations in the U.S.. He is a butcher and Kelly is a school teacher. All of the Tacketts worship and serve at Antioch Church where Pete pastors.

"I have no greater joy than to hear that my children are walking in the truth." 3 John 1:4

Michael D. Stover

Michael D. Stover is a husband to one, father of five, proud grandfather, and a cancer survivor. Since 2005, he has written, edited, and contributed to numerous bible study materials, college subject matter, blogs, websites, fiction, poetry, and nonfiction works. He holds degrees from Union University and Mid-America Baptist Theological Seminary, both in his home state of Tennessee.

Michael's experience in vocational Christian ministry includes serving as youth pastor, assistant pastor, minister of missions, education, & evangelism, and senior pastor at churches in Mississippi and Tennessee from 1993-2013.

He has also served as an association Sunday School Director, Association VBS Director, Area Crusade Outreach Leader, National VBS Training Team Member for LifeWay Christian Resources in 2007-2008, TN Baptist VBS Training Team Member in 2005, 2007, 2008, MS Baptist VBS Training Team Member in 2008, as well as a writer for numerous VBS and Adult Sunday School resources for LifeWay Christian Resources.

Michael has published *How to Write Well*, a self-help book to assist aspiring writers in improving their craft; and *Jesus and Dirt: A Fresh Look at the Parable of the Sower*, a bible study resource for small groups and pastors. Both resources are available in print, digital, and audiobook versions.

In addition to full-time freelance writing and editing, Michael enjoys reading, fishing, cooking, beaches, old movies, history, 80s music, and lots of family time. Visit his website at www.michaeldstover.com.